THE MENDED ROSE

By

Rosalee & T. Christopher Jarrell

ISBN: 0-75963-047-X

This book is printed on acid free paper.

1stBooks - rev. 04/25/01

INTRODUCTION

While the subject matter of this book, specifically rape and child abuse, would seem an adult matter, the fact that it <u>does</u> happen to children shows that anyone of any age can benefit from reading my wife's story. Her triumph over tragedy should inspire any who have suffered abuse to achieve victory over their past.

Our purpose in writing this book is not to discourage people from becoming foster parents, nor is it to condemn the foster care system. On the contrary, we urge people who are full of love, character, and virtue to become foster parents. We also encourage the adoption of needy children and teens. As for the foster care system, we only want it to follow its own precautions so that, hopefully, what happened to Rose will not happen again.

We are also <u>not</u> trying to get revenge on the person who abused Rose. Since these events occurred, we have talked to him. Though he has not apologized, or even admitted that what he did was wrong, we would like to offer forgiveness to him. We have forgiven him in our hearts, but, as far as we know, he has not accepted it. As an attempt at reconciliation, we asked him to do some construction work for us, since he does that as a side job. At first he accepted, but later declined. The inability to accept forgiveness from both God and others is as terrible a thing as abuse. Our hearts go out to the abused and the abusers. God can restore the abused and forgive the abusers. We hope this book will show both how they can draw closer to God.

Sincerely,

T. Christopher Jarrell

CHAPTER ONE

She lay in her bed shivering with fear, a sense of nausea and dread hanging over her, crushing her. She knew that any minute now *he* would sneak into her room and make her do those terrible things that made her so ashamed. She wishes she could die. If only she had been born a boy, none of this would have happened to her. She would not be living in a constant nightmare. "Dear God, why didn't you make me a boy? Why did I have to be a girl?"

She is nude, of course, just as he commanded. Her lip still hurts from the blow he had given her when she said she would not have sex with him. She always said no, but he always forced her anyway. She was only safe at school, unless he came and picked her up early. She knew if her name was called over the intercom it was him wanting to take her home and rape her again before his wife got home from work.

Almost nightly, as soon as everyone else was asleep, he would sneak in to her room to force her to have sex again. The only exception was during her period. Then, she could relax. Another month had gone by and he hadn't gotten her pregnant. Then her body could purge itself of his filth and she could sleep a little more easily for five nights or so.

For a while, she had shared a bedroom with her foster sister, Stephanie, so he had not forced her in that room. Now that she had her own bedroom, though, even it was no longer a safe haven. Before she had her own bedroom, he would make her stay up while everyone else went to bed. Then he would rape her in the living room.

"Why doesn't somebody wake up and find us?" she wondered. Before she had gotten the new bedroom, all it would have taken was for someone to wake up and have to go to the bathroom. Then they would have found them both naked in the living room. Nobody ever did, though. Once Linda, her foster mother, had gone to sleep, she never woke till the morning. After all these years, surely she would have missed her husband's presence in bed with her and wondered where he was. She never let on that she did.

Stephanie was no help, either. Jerry, Rose's foster father, and Stephanie's biological father, had been molesting his own daughter before Rose came. She had not told Rose this before Rose had come to live with them. She had not warned Rose what kind of evil man Jerry was. Rose was completely unprepared for what was to become a waking nightmare for the six or so years she would live with the D___s.

Jerry had left Stephanie alone once Rose came to live with them. He felt better raping a foster child than molesting his own daughter. "At least Rose isn't really my daughter," he thought, "so it can't be as bad." This is what he convinced himself.

Rose confronted Stephanie after the first time. Stephanie even took her father's side, spouting the same rationales he had tried to tell Rose. Stephanie was completely brainwashed. She could not even see that what Jerry was doing to them was wrong. She did whatever her father asked; obeyed whatever he said; agreed with every excuse he gave, no matter how irrational. Little did Rose realize, but in the next months, she would become *almost* as thoroughly brainwashed. Still, she would never accept it as right, nor would she submit to his sexual advances willingly. "Dear God, please get me out of here!" she would often pray.

Chris was twelve and living in Monticello, Georgia. He had noticed a feeling of uneasiness lately. A sense of loneliness was around him constantly. He had a few friends, and a pretty good home life, but still he felt lonely. He felt an urgent need to pray for his future wife.

"Lord Jesus," he prayed, "please bring me a wife in Your time. I know I am too young to get married now, but I know You have someone picked out for me. I feel that she is hurting and needing help. Lord, please protect her. Bless her, and wrap Your love around her. Let her feel Your presence around her and comfort her. Let her know that I love her, too, and that I'll be glad to be her husband. In Jesus' name, Amen."

As he was about to enter the ninth grade, he recalled that he had never had an "official" girlfriend. Most girls made fun of him and called him names. There had been one girl, though. She had moved in across the street. They had been close, though only knowing each other during the summer several years before. She had tried to get him to go in the woods for something she called "sex." He didn't know what that was, but she said it had something to do with taking each other's clothes off and that it would be fun.

When she said that, something in his body began to tingle. He was suddenly very happy and felt a sense of excitement, as if it was his birthday and it was finally time to open the presents.

As they were standing on the sidewalk in front of his house, she eagerly awaiting an answer, he made up his mind that he **would** go in the woods with her and try this thing she called "sex." Just as the "yes" he wanted to give was about to fall out of his mouth, doing a swan dive off the tip of his tongue, he heard a loud voice sternly say "No!" He looked around expecting to see either his Dad or hers close by with a foul, angry expression on his face. Chris fully expected to be grounded, as would the cute, twelve-year-old little temptress. There was nobody in sight in any direction. As he was looking he realized that voice didn't sound like either parent. Then, he remembered the story in the Bible of Samuel the prophet.

Samuel was serving in the temple under Eli. His mother, Hannah, had taken him to live in the temple with this priest soon after he was weaned. She was giving Samuel back to God in thanks for allowing her to have a child after she had been barren for years.

Samuel heard a voice while sleeping that was calling his name. He thought it was Eli and ran to the sleeping priest asking what he needed. Eli told him to go back to bed; he must have been dreaming. Samuel lay back down and again heard a voice say "Samuel." When he again ran to the priest, asking why Eli needed him, Eli realized it must be God speaking to the child. He told Samuel, "The voice you heard was the Lord God. Go back to bed and when you again hear the voice calling you, say, 'Speak, Lord, for Your servant is listening,' and do whatever He says."

Chris realized the voice he was hearing must be God's, too, but he said nothing to the girl standing before him, who was *still* waiting patiently for an answer. Instead, just like a child who is told he can't have the candy on the shelf right in front of him at the grocery store check out line, he pleaded with God, without saying a word aloud, "But... I... waaaaant... tooooo!"

Again, the voice, louder and more sternly this time, said, "No!!," like a parent asserting his proper authority over a child, which child would do anything regardless of consequences if ignorant of the dangers and if that thing looked sufficiently appealing.

Chris remembered how a few years back, at age six, to be exact, he had been sitting at church doing what he always had done—fidgeting and listening to absolutely nothing the preacher was saying. His parents had taken him to church for as long as he could remember. Many parents send their children to church, but his actually went with him and stayed. They weren't the kind that had to be in church every time the doors were open. They would go to church and be there Sunday morning, Sunday night, and Wednesday night for a couple of months, then go only to Sunday morning services for about four to six months, then back to every service. His parents prayed with the children about as sporadically, but they finally stopped after a while, though they never stopped going to church in their weird cycle.

Before age six, he had done just like the other children—fidget, whisper, and giggle with the other children, and crawl under the pews from the back of the church to almost the front. They would never go all the way to the front because then they might get spotted by the pastor, or the deacons, or even his Mom in the choir and then they would surely get in trouble. Trouble meant a whipping, and he tried to avoid those whenever possible.

They never beat him. He never considered spankings as abuse, mainly because they weren't. He always deserved every whipping, and they only spanked his bottom. There was plenty of natural padding there, and it never hurt long, anyway.

As they intended, he never repeated the sin for which he had received the spanking, so they were getting more rare the older he got, and the more he

3

learned how to behave in public—not to "lie, cheat, steal, cuss, or beat up your little brother and sister." His older sister, though, never learned that last lesson when it concerned him, and Chris has to admit, it was well into high school before he learned it.

He found himself at age six at Enon Baptist church, several miles outside of Monticello on the road to Forsyth and on the way to Macon. He was not listening as usual. They had been having a week of revival meetings, and this was the last night. A guest preacher had been preaching every night, but Chris had paid him the same attention as he had the pastor—none.

He couldn't tell you a single word the preacher had said all week. He didn't know if anyone had come forward to accept Jesus as Lord and Savior. He didn't even know the preacher's name. All he knew was that the preacher looked funny. He was several years (maybe even decades) younger than his white-haired pastor. The guest preacher was short and skinny, with curly hair that looked much like a small Afro, though the man was white. He also wore glasses with round lenses and frames—"John Lennon" glasses, as Chris would call them later. He was not an intimidating character, to put it politely.

Here Chris was, sitting on the left side of the church (left as you enter, not from the pulpit), in the second row. Only the pastor and the really holy people sat in the front seat. The choir director had made his son sit in the second row, so Chris, not wanting to be bored the whole service, sat there with him and a few other boys.

They were all whispering and giggling. The pastor would sometimes turn around and wave his hand below the level of the back of the pew, so the whole church wouldn't see, in a motion that meant "keep it down." They would also get stern looks from the father of the boy who seemed to be loudest at the moment. The looks meant, "keep it up and you'll be in trouble when we get home," and everyone already knows what that means.

The children who were old enough, including Chris, had just sung a song for the church so the parents could puff out their chests and look around, wanting to say, "That's my child," but not daring to utter a word. Of course, there were the usual "Awww"'s and whispered "Aren't they so cute'"s.

The children sang a song using the letters of the word "Christian," but Chris didn't know the whole song, or what it meant. All he knew was his line and that he was supposed to start when the person beside him stopped. When the song was completed, the children went to sit down. The choir director directed his son to the second row and Chris, partly not wanting to be bored and partly not wanting to walk all the way back to his seat while all those adults watched him do it, quickly followed the other boy, as did several more boys.

It was time for the sermon to be preached by the preacher and ignored by the boys. Almost at the very end though, something happened that had never happened before. For some unknown reason, Chris began to listen to the preacher, without meaning to do so. The other boys soon tired of trying to regain Chris' attention. Chris could see them playing out of the corner of his eye, but his attention was now focused on the preacher and what he was saying. The preacher was talking about Jesus on the cross and why Jesus was willing to sacrifice Himself for us.

Some object to Christianity because they think God the Father put His Son to death and this repulses them. In reality, God the Father stood by and watched because Jesus was **willing** to give Himself as a sacrifice so that people might have the opportunity to go to heaven. God the Father wanted to intervene and would have, except that Jesus never asked Him to intervene. Hebrews says that for the joy set before Him, Jesus endured the cross. The joy that was set before Him was us—humanity.

If Adam and Eve had not chosen to obey Satan and disobey God, thereby committing the first human sin and immediately incurring the penalty for sin— spiritual death (which is separation from God), with the resulting consequence of physical death following years later, then Jesus would not have needed to die in our place. We would never have died nor needed a Savior.

As the first humans, though, they started the cycle of sin that would follow all humans since then. Just as an alcoholic parent raises a child who, though objecting to alcoholism all along, becomes an alcoholic, so we are sinners because our parents are sinners and so on back to Adam and Eve.

When we are judged to determine if we can go to heaven, we are not compared to other people, as most assume, but we are judged according to the true standard, God himself. Thus, nobody is ever good enough to enter heaven, because nobody is as good as God Himself.

Knowing our dilemma, Jesus, in the eternity before time ever began, determined that when the world would be created, and knowing that humanity would choose to sin and be under a death penalty, He would enter our dimensions of time and space to take that penalty on Himself. But since a human did the crime, a human had to pay the penalty. That is why the animal sacrifices in the Old Testament were temporary and had to be repeated—they only delayed the punishment, not fulfill it. Only a human could appease the penalty for sin. But, since all humans are sinners by heredity, none could be good enough to pay the penalty, and being only human, one person's death would not be acceptable for all humans.

Jesus, being God, had to become human, also, without ceasing to be deity. Only humanity could pay the penalty, but only deity could make that payment valuable enough to transfer to the accounts of all humans ever born. This was why the incarnation was necessary. Still, even though Jesus paid the penalty for everyone for all eternity, that payment is not credited to our account to pay for our individual penalties until we accept Him personally as our Lord and Savior, asking Him to change us, trusting Him to do what is best for us, trusting that His death on the cross did, in fact, pay our penalty, and obeying Him when He tells us to do something or not to do something.

Chris sat listening to the description of Jesus on the cross—the crown of thorns on His bleeding head, the torn places in His flesh from the bone-laced whip, the nails which pierced His hands and feet, the gaping hole in His side from a Roman spear which pierced His heart. Suddenly, Chris could no longer see the boys playing around him, the pastor seated in front of him, the preacher behind the pulpit, nor even the church building. He could no longer hear the preacher.

Chris felt himself transported almost 2,000 years previously. He was standing on a dusty patch of ground looking around. There were no plants growing anywhere. The sky was a reddish purple, as if the sky itself were bleeding and the clouds were black with soaking up so much blood. The thunder was rolling in the distance, and then Chris' eyes fell upon the cross, seeing Jesus just as the preacher had described. Chris suddenly felt very sad.

Then, Jesus lifted His badly bruised and lacerated head and looked at Chris directly. He forced out the words, "I love you." Chris felt immediately immersed in love. It was as if someone had wrapped a warm blanket around him on a cold day. The warmth and love Chris felt were beyond description—more than he has experienced before or since.

"I love You, too!" Chris shouted, now weeping uncontrollably. "Oh, Jesus! I'm sorry that you had to die for me! I know I've lied before. I have said mean things to and about my Mom, Dad, and grandparents. I've been mean to my brother and sister. Please forgive me! I don't want to hurt You ever again. I don't want You to be disappointed with me. I love You!"

Instantly, Chris found himself back in church. The preacher was no longer preaching behind the pulpit, but was standing before the congregation in front of the pulpit, inviting anyone who wanted to ask Jesus into his or her heart to come to the front and let him pray with that person to ask Jesus to be his Lord and Savior.

Chris wanted to go forward, but wouldn't. He had missed everything the preacher had said between describing Jesus on the cross and that moment. He wasn't sure he understood what he was supposed to do. Beside that, he realized that though he was crying uncontrollably in his vision of the Lord, his eyes were still dry. His lip was quivering, and he knew that if he walked up front he would start crying like he was in the vision. Since "boys don't cry," he just held tighter to the pew in front of him, forcing himself to be still and not to cry. Also, he didn't want to go in front of all those people. What would they think of him? He imagined he would be all embarrassed.

The invitation ended and the congregation sang the last verse of "Just As I Am" for the twentieth and final time. Chris still had not moved toward that carpeted aisle leading to the waiting preacher. It was blood red carpet that looked like Astroturf and lined the center aisle, the area across the front of the church, and the platform where the pulpit and choir's seats were. He saw the same carpet in many other churches that he would visit over the years. "Are all Baptist churches required to buy the same color and kind of carpet? Do they all shop at the same store?" he would one day wonder.

The preacher looked at Chris. "Does he know that I just saw Jesus?" Chris wondered.

People started gathering Bibles, purses, and children, preparing to leave. Chris made his way past the preacher and the adults socializing in the aisles. He went through the door between the organ and the platform, which door led to the fellowship hall behind the sanctuary. He stepped down into the hallway, made an immediate left, then right, and went into the first door on the right—the nursery. The last child had just been picked up and the nursery lady was leaving. He shut the door a few seconds after she left. He went and sat down on the floor against the far wall. He sat between an adult-sized rocking chair and an empty crib, gathering his knees up to his chest and laying his head on his arms, which were on his knees. Now he could cry. Nobody could see him. The only problem was, now that he had started, he couldn't stop.

"I'm sorry, Jesus. I know you wanted me to go forward and ask you to come into my heart. I could feel you pushing me to go. I'm sorry I didn't obey you, and just when I said I never wanted to hurt you again. Please forgive me."

Chris sat there crying for what seemed to him to be hours. His older sister, Melanie, opened the door enough to put her head into the room and see her brother crying.

"What's wrong?" she asked. He was crying too much to answer her. He just looked at her, helplessly. She knew that Chris usually only cried for a few reasons: she had beaten him up; he had gotten another spanking; or he had gotten hurt pretty badly—usually on his bicycle. She knew none of these had happened at church, and he could still talk through the tears if they had, so this had to be something serious.

She shut the door behind her, not saying another word. She ran to find Mom and Dad. They came and asked him what was wrong. He could only say he had wanted to go forward and ask Jesus to come into his heart, but didn't, and that he had hurt Jesus. Dad went to find the pastor. Mom did as all moms do who love their children—she stayed and hugged her little boy, trying to comfort her "baby." Ordinarily, Chris would have objected to this. He wasn't a "baby" any more, after all. He was six years old! Tonight, though, he didn't mind.

Dad returned with the pastor and the guest preacher. They asked him what was wrong. He explained again why he was crying. After questioning him thoroughly to ascertain that he understood what salvation meant, the pastor led Chris in a prayer to ask Jesus to be his Lord and Savior.

Chris wasn't worried about dying and going to Hell. He was not worried about "fire insurance," nor did he only want to be "saved" as a "fire escape" from Hell, as people are accused of doing when they go forward and say a prayer, though they never try to change and nothing ever comes from their actions. Such prayers do no good anyway. Only a prayer of sincere repentance and commitment to Jesus, not to a church or a preacher, but to God himself, will help a person.

Escaping Hell was not Chris' motive for wanting to ask Jesus to be his Lord and Savior. No, Chris' motive was out of a pure and sincere love for the one who died for him even though he didn't deserve it.

It was this love for his Savior that kept him from sinning when he realized that such actions hurt the heart of his Lord. Oh, he still committed sins and still does. After all, nobody is perfect but Jesus. His love for Jesus, though, is so strong that when he realizes that what he is doing is sin, he stops doing it and asks for forgiveness and refuses to do it again.

Having remembered all this and knowing that his love for Jesus was stronger than even his love for his family, or his desire to find out what this thing the little girl called "sex" was, he decided to obey Jesus. He turned to the cute girl who was still looking at him awaiting an answer and simply said, "I can't." That was the end of the discussion. She moved away before school started that fall.

Little did Chris realize that he would soon see her again, as she would return in a few days when he entered the ninth grade. He regretted his decision not to have sex with her for several years, until he met his future wife. It was then he understood why God had said no to him several years before. He had known this little girl was not to be his wife, but since she was the only one who was ever interested in him until his senior year of high school, he had hoped it would be her to whom he would wed.

When God had told him at age twelve to pray for his future wife, he knew it was another girl, not the one who wanted to have sex with him a few days before. That girl, for whom he prayed asking God to protect her and comfort her, was beginning to go through a trial unimaginable to him; one that he would not learn about until many years later.

CHAPTER TWO

Rose was almost asleep. "Maybe he forgot," she hoped, knowing he had not. She felt an evil, demonic presence fill her room seconds before he opened the door. He took off his clothes and walked over to her bed. He started to pull the cover off of her naked body. She tried to hold it, but he yanked it out of her hand.

He was well over six feet tall, muscular, but with a large belly. He had dark hair with a menacing, intimidating presence and a stern face. He gave orders to all members of his family and expected immediate compliance. With her, though, what he wanted was her body.

She was five feet tall, anemic, barely ninety pounds. There was a sharp pain when he forced himself into her and a dull pain throughout intercourse, lasting several minutes after he finished. He never tried to excite her sexually before beginning. He never asked her if it hurt. He never cared. He was only concerned with himself. He never wore a condom, refused to let her use birth control, and only rarely used any kind of lubricant.

Only rarely did he say anything to her, except to call her a whore and tell her again that she had better not tell anyone or he would "get her." He never explained what he meant by that, but it terrified her. She used to bleed from his rapings, but he had done it so many times now that she didn't bleed, but she still hurt.

She never moved while he was in her. She didn't participate. She never said anything, didn't kiss him, never reached her arms for him. She lay there perfectly still, like a plastic blow-up doll. "He might take my body by force, but no matter what, he can't have my mind," she thought.

To cope, her mind would block out what he was doing to her while he was there. Her mind would wander anywhere. It didn't matter where, as long as she wasn't thinking about what he was doing to her.

Life had not always been like this for her. Her mind went back to her early childhood, forgetting his presence and the harm he was doing to her.

Rose began life as the daughter of an alcoholic father. He would get drunk and hit various members of the family. Her mother finally left him when Rose was two years old. Rose would only see her real father a couple of times in her life before he died years later.

Rose was the youngest of four children. Her grandmother was allowed to name the last child and she chose 'Rosalee' with no middle name. Her grandmother was a full-blooded Cherokee and said the name meant "giver of love," saying that even in the crib, Rose was full of joy and love. Little did anyone realize that like her Cherokee ancestors, Rose would have to travel down her own "Trail of Tears." Her grandmother called her "My Little Rose," a name her future husband would call her even before he discovered that her beloved grandmother had called her the same thing.

To support her children, Rose's mother became a go-go dancer. Rose only saw her mother on Sundays. For the rest of the week, the children stayed with a baby-sitter. Now, Rose does not remember her Mom at all from those early years. All she remembers is a blue-eyed woman with a bun hair-do.

Her mother was an exotic dancer until Rose was four. Then she met a customer who decided he wanted to marry her and help her with her children. He took good care of them, providing income through a mechanic's wages. Her mother became a laundry worker at a nearby hospital.

Their first house, located in Rockmart, burned because of faulty wiring. It was a house that her father was trying to remodel.

Rose's new adoptive father and her mother then bought a motel. At this time, the eldest child, Cheryl, came back to live with her siblings, though she would repeatedly run away. She had been taken into foster care because of her alcoholic father. Rose had not met her until this time, and did not know why Cheryl kept running away.

Rose and her older sister, Donna, shared a room. Their brother, Randy, had his own room, and Cheryl had one to herself as well. Rose enjoyed this time.

Later, they rented a home in Buchanan. Rose's mother began to have unexplained mood swings, changing from angry to happy in a matter of seconds. One evening, her father had to work late. It was an anniversary and he was unable to take his wife out to dinner as he had promised. Instead, he brought her flowers. She accused him of having an affair and sleeping around, though this was the first time he was ever late. She told him that he was no good and of no account. All of this was untrue.

The next day, she was very nice to him and didn't remember anything from the night before, not even what she had said. These should have been warning signs of an oncoming mental illness, but nobody understood what was going on.

When Rose was eleven, Rose's mother had her husband arrested for molesting her daughters, but Rose doesn't remember a single incident of it. She absolutely doesn't believe that her adoptive father did anything of which he was accused and bears no ill will against him. She realizes that this was probably just her mother's mental illness increasing.

Her mother had the girls tested for possible sexual abuse. Her father spent very little time in prison (less than two months), confirming to Rose that the accusations against him were false and imagined. Still, her father could not face what was happening to his wife, so he granted her the divorce for which she asked, even agreeing not to contact the girls until after Rose, the youngest, turned eighteen.

Rose and the other children did not know what their mother was doing. They thought their father was abandoning them when they needed him most, and that he didn't love them.

A week after she had him incarcerated, Rose's mother visited him in the jail and said she was sorry. She did not know why she said those things about him. She said she did not know what she was doing and that she did not mean it, but the damage was done. Rose was now in the fifth grade.

Her mother began hallucinating soon afterwards. While driving down the road, she would tell her children, "I know those people. I went to school with them." The children saw no one, and when they questioned her on the matter, she remained silent.

Her mother became worried that she would be unable, financially, to care for the children. They moved, therefore, from the rental house in Buchanan to government housing in Cedartown, where she began receiving government assistance.

At this time, her mind completely left her. The children took on ever-increasing responsibilities, including dishes, laundry, cleaning, cooking, and even filling out the paperwork to renew Medicaid and Food stamps while just letting their mother sign the papers. If the children had their doors closed, she would bang on the doors, and if they didn't immediately open them, she would run outside and break their window to get in. She was imagining them committing suicide or doing drugs.

They saw their mother deteriorate from a normal adult mother to the status of an infant. They had to bathe, dress, and feed her. They had to escort her to the bathroom and help her, or else she would just go on the floor wherever she happened to be. Rose had to sleep with her so that if she got up during the night, Rose could follow and make sure that she didn't get hurt, but that she did what she needed to do and went back to bed. Donna quit school to care for her during the day while Rose went to school because Rose was only twelve.

Somebody called Rose's aunt and she finally came and discovered the circumstances under which the children were living. The aunt, Ann, tried to get help for her sister, but finally had her committed to a mental institution. Cheryl had long since married and vanished. Donna married at sixteen and was living with her husband. Randy was old enough to be on his own. Rose, who was in the sixth grade, was not old enough to go on her own.

Ann took Rose home with her, but as she had two teenage boys of her own, she was wary lest any mischief be committed. She tried to find a place for Rose. It was becoming ever more apparent to Rose that nobody wanted her, though she had shown great responsibility in caring for her mother. Desperate to be rid of her niece, Ann decided to make up lies about her.

First, she took Rose to a mental institution and tried to have her committed, but Rose was not insane. Ann also took her to a drug rehab center for teens, but

Rose was no addict. She had never even had any drugs, and so, wasn't accepted. She finally found an organization that cared for abused and unwanted children and left her there, not contacting Rose for over a decade.

This organization had a large main campus and several smaller homes, called relief shelters. Rose was taken to one of the shelters, this one in a place called "Dewey Rose." The directors of the shelter were named Mike and Denise. They were very kind to all the children. Most of the time, Rose shared a room with two other girls. Only if there were no other girls could Rose get a room to herself.

She, like all the children, was only supposed to be there for thirty days. Since Rose had nowhere to go of which she knew, she was left there on a long-term basis. The other children went home for holidays, but the directors, Mike and Denise, had to take Rose with them for the holidays.

By this time, Rose was really beginning to have trouble with protruding upper teeth, "buck teeth" as they were commonly known. This was a result of the incorrect use of calipers to extract Rose from her mother's birth canal. This embarrassed Rose. Since her mother had been divorced, she had been forced to wear old, cheap, out-of-date clothing, causing her constant teasing by classmates. Her self-esteem was sinking the older she became.

Mike and Denise, like the good Christians they were, always treated Rose well, like one of the family. She wasn't made to feel like an outsider when she did have to go with them on vacations. They were always kind to her, for which she is still appreciative. They accepted her for who she was, despite her looks and her dress. They would take the children who were staying there at the shelter to church on Sundays in Royston or Hartwell. They had nightly devotions and prayer with the children.

Each child was assigned a chore to complete each day, to teach them responsibility and keeping a schedule. Such duties included washing clothes or dishes and cleaning up after themselves. Rose had no problem with this because she was doing all of it when her mother lost her mind from a chemical imbalance. Rose went to school down the road, where it ended into the road that went from Hartwell to Royston. It was at this school, Eagle Grove Middle School, that she met Stephanie and became friends with her, though Stephanie hid from Rose a dark secret. Rose was now in the seventh grade.

When Stephanie found out that children at the shelter could have visitors, she began coming to see Rose. There was a play area in front of the shelter; and in the upstairs part of the shelter, there was a playroom. Stephanie and Rose spent a lot of time together that year and during the summer. Rose thought she was a nice, and very sweet, girl. Stephanie wouldn't talk much about her family, though.

Stephanie finally got up the courage to ask if Rose could come stay with her and her family one weekend. Mike and Denise asked their supervisors, and got permission for Rose to spend a Sunday with the D___s. They went to a small, Pentecostal-type church a few miles away. They asked Rose why she was at the shelter and what the children did while they were there. Rose came over a few Sundays after that.

Shortly, the D___s began to help out at the shelter, becoming relief help workers so that Mike and Denise could have time for themselves for the sake of their marriage. Jerry and Linda said they felt sorry for Rose and wanted to help her. They got accustomed to each other on the weekends the D___s performed their duties as relief help. She and Stephanie would talk for hours, but still Stephanie said nothing about her secret.

Rose started staying with the D___s more and more, until, by November of her eighth grade year, she was living with them. Jerry and Linda had three children— Stephanie, who was a year younger than the now fifteen-year-old Rose, and Greg and Brian, both of whom were younger than Stephanie. They made this foster child feel at home at first, and they were still relief helping, though less and less. After a time, they quit altogether. Nobody at the shelter knew what was going on in that home, however. All appearances showed that they were a normal family.

For a foster child to begin living with foster parents, paperwork is supposed to be filled out by the foster parents, submitted, reviewed, and approved by the child care organization, and sometimes by DFACS (the Department of Family and Children's Services), which is responsible for taking children out of abusive homes and putting them in safe care. Afterwards, a home inspection and interview should be conducted before a child is ever allowed to enter a foster home. None of this occurred in Rose's case.

Because Rose had been at the relief shelter for over a year, instead of the usual thirty days, everyone was in a rush when there was finally an offer for someone to accept a teenager. Children are usually easier to place in foster homes than teenagers. Few people want to deal with their own teenagers, much less someone else's, and even less one that has stayed in a children's home, regardless of whether the child has done anything wrong or not. Jerry had no criminal record or reports of child molestation, so he was assumed to be safe. Having helped out at the shelter for the past few months helped him masquerade further as a good, loving parent instead of the monster he truly was.

When Rose went to live with the D___s permanently, she saw the paperwork on the kitchen table, still unfilled. She never knew if they ever filled it out and submitted it later, but they had not done it before that time, as the rules stated. No home inspection was conducted, either. Rose was simply introduced to the D___s, but she already knew their names.

The child care organization was even more eager to place Rose anywhere, because her long-term paperwork, which allowed her to stay with that organization, was coming due and would have to be filed to DFACS again. The relief shelter was filling, and the main campus, which did house long-term foster children, but not teenagers as yet, still had no room for Rose, as it had not for the past year. It would be so much easier to place her in foster care, and the D___s were the first ones in over a year who were willing to accept a teenager into their home. Also, the organization thought it would be better to place Rose in a home with a girl her own age instead of keeping her in shelters on the main campus with children younger than she was. After all, what teenager enjoys spending all their time with little kids?

CHAPTER THREE

Her first night living with the D___s was pretty uneventful. She was introduced to Jerry and Linda, Stephanie, Greg, and Brian (though, again, she already knew their names). She was shown the room she would be sharing with Stephanie (though she had already stayed there a few times). They showed her around the house. They lived on one hundred sixty acres, though Jerry's mom owned it. Rose would be attending the same school that she had been attending, Eagle Grove Middle School, which now is only an elementary school, though then it also housed the middle school. She would also be riding the bus with Stephanie, so everything seemed wonderful.

For two weeks, things went well. They all celebrated Thanksgiving together. Rose began to think that she would finally have a happy family life again. How mistaken she was!

At the end of the second week, Jerry was sitting in his usual chair. Everyone else, except he and Rose, was busy in other rooms and probably would not return anytime soon. He told her to come sit in his lap. She had known them for several months by this time, including the two weeks she had lived with them, and he had never made any sexual advances toward her. Stephanie had never warned her about Jerry, and Rose had seen Stephanie and the boys at various times sit in Jerry's lap, so she felt she could trust him. She thought nothing about his request.

She crawled onto his lap, and he asked her to tell him her story. She talked about her mother losing her mind and how her aunt had not wanted her. She told of how she had lived at the shelter for so long and that the D___s were the only people even to say they wanted a teenager to come and live with them.

"Why are you coming onto me sexually?" he interrupted.

"Huh?" she replied. She wasn't saying anything about sex. She was just being obedient to him by sitting in his lap and telling him her story like he had told her to do.

"You're coming onto me by sitting in my lap," he said, though he was the one who had told her to do it. "And why are you wearing such tight clothes? You look so sexy in them. You shouldn't wear clothes like that."

She was wearing her usual attire of a baggy T-shirt and shorts, which were acceptable school attire in warmer weather. Now, she wore them around the house most afternoons. The shorts weren't even short-shorts. Like what she wears today, they were loose fitting, not tight, and went all the way to her knees. She couldn't understand what he was calling tight fitting. With her "buck teeth," her anemic, bony appearance (barely ninety pounds, even when she graduated high school years later), and casual clothing, she didn't see how anyone thought she looked "sexy." She certainly didn't think she was. She didn't even think she was pretty.

Afraid of offending her new host and being kicked out again as her aunt had done to her, she pleaded, "Well, what do you want me to do?"

"I don't want you to do anything," he answered. "My wife and I are having problems sexually. She's as loose as a wet noodle. That comes from having children. She doesn't satisfy me sexually anymore. Rose, I want to have sex with you."

"I don't want to have sex with you. I don't believe in that. I've accepted Jesus Christ as my Lord and Savior, and I don't believe in that," she blurted, horrified.

"You have to have sex with me or move out. You know you don't have anywhere else to go. Your aunt doesn't want you, and the childcare people don't have anywhere else for you. Where else are you going to go? You will have sex with me." He didn't try to touch her that day, but kept telling her for the next few days that she would have to have sex with him because she had nowhere else to go.

She began to believe him. She knew, too, that her aunt did not want her and the organization that placed her in Jerry's home had nowhere else for her. She was terrified that she would be kicked out and end up starving to death in the woods.

The shelter was only a few miles away, but she knew it was full. She didn't think they could find anywhere for her, since they had not been able to find anywhere for her in the past year.

The nearest neighbors other than the shelter were miles away, and she thought if she went there, they would just call Jerry and he would come get her and beat her for doing it. Everything appeared hopeless.

The whole two weeks she had been there, Jerry had gotten her to massage his forehead because of the migraine headaches he was having. He would lie on the sofa and have her kneel on the floor at the end of the sofa and massage his head until he fell asleep, similar to the Biblical account of David playing his harp to soothe the troubled King Saul.

A few days after he had told her that she would have to have sex with him, he called to her from his bedroom, "Rose, come here. I have a headache and I need you to massage it."

She walked in, expecting to see him lying on the bed with his head at the foot of the bed. She assumed that she would kneel on the floor and massage his head so he could sleep. She was puzzled when she saw the bed empty. "I thought he called me from in here," she thought.

She heard the door shut and lock behind her. She spun around to see him standing in front of it. As he pulled down his pants, he repeated that she knew she had nowhere else to go and that she would starve on her own. "I told you

you were going to have sex with me. Now put your mouth right here," he said, pointing to his penis.

She hesitated, frightened and not wanting to do what he was asking her to do. He straightened his back and looked angrily at her. He was a foot and a half taller than she was and outweighed her by two hundred pounds. She was nowhere near his strength. He looked very much like a giant grizzly bear ready to kill someone who had been unfortunate enough to stumble upon it. As a grizzly can kill a human with a well-aimed swipe of the paw, he looked like he could easily kill her. She was terrified even more than before, afraid to obey, but even more afraid not to obey.

She knelt down in front of him. "Do it!" he ordered. He had to give her instructions as she went along because she had never done this before. His anger subsided as she continued and he began to relax, becoming more talkative.

"I don't really want to have sex with you. It's just that I'm so horny and I need relief from all of this tension," he said, trying to make it sound like what he was forcing her to do was not all that bad. He tried to convince her that she was, after all, helping him.

He showed her his collection of Playboys and Penthouses. "This is my private stash," he said. "This is how I've been relieving myself before now," he said, showing her the pictures of the naked women. Rose could not have cared less. She just wanted to be out of there.

"Nobody else knows about these," he stated. As he made her continue, he confided, "Stephanie has done this for me a few times, but we never have had sex."

After he finished, Rose confronted Stephanie. "Why didn't you tell me what your father was doing? He just made me suck on his penis! How disgusting! I never would have come here if you had told me he was doing that to you. Now, it's too late and I have nowhere else to go. I'm trapped. Why didn't you tell me?" Rose demanded.

"I was hoping he wouldn't do that with you. I thought he would have more respect for you since you are a foster child."

"Why are you doing it? You can go live with any of your aunts or uncles, or anybody. I can't."

"I love my daddy. He needs help. He explained the situation to me. Mom no longer satisfies him sexually because she is too loose from having children. He has all this tension and needs relief from it," Stephanie said, regurgitating the same rationalizations that Jerry had given Rose. "I'm praying that God will deliver him from it. Besides, we haven't been doing it long—only a few times."

Stephanie would be no help at all. In the six years that were to follow, when Jerry would rape Rose repeatedly, Stephanie would not try to protect Rose or prevent it. She would report it to no one.

After six months to a year, Jerry would stop with Stephanie altogether in favor of Rose, doing worse things to Rose than he had ever done to Stephanie. Still, Stephanie would tell no one.

Perhaps Stephanie was just so selfish that she dare not say anything lest Rose be taken away and he start back with her. Was she only concerned with herself? Or, perhaps, she really believed her dad would get better someday. Or, did she agree with her father that his having sex with a foster child wasn't as bad as having sex with his own daughter?

Rose was "only a foster child," after all. Maybe, somehow, raping one girl isn't as sinful as raping another girl? To humans, this may have seemed correct, but not to God. Stephanie would not talk to Rose about what was going on again, ever.

When she went to college and had no need to fear retaliation from her father, she still would not say anything or try to help Rose. When Stephanie got engaged to be married, she wouldn't even tell her fiancé.

"Aren't you going to tell him what Jerry did to you? Don't you think he should know since he is going to be your husband?" Rose asked.

"No, I want Dad and him to have a good relationship and if I told him he would hate Dad."

"But what if y'all have children? Aren't you afraid you might have a daughter? You know you can't leave her alone with Jerry or let her come spend the night with her grandparents. Doesn't that bother you?"

"I'll worry about that later," Stephanie said, ending the conversation.

Years later, when Jerry would finally be found out and Rose was removed from that home, Stephanie still offered no help. She even begged Rose not to send her father to prison.

CHAPTER FOUR

For the next few weeks, he repeatedly forced Rose to perform oral sex on him. As is the case when one dabbles in pornography, there comes a time when the "milder stuff" no longer excites a person, and he must either give up his habit or go to the "harder stuff" to achieve the same results as before, so oral sex became unexciting to Jerry. Instead of giving up molesting Rose and Stephanie, he chose to begin having sex with Rose and letting Stephanie perform oral sex on him when Rose was on her "monthly."

When Jerry first began making Rose have oral sex with him, and for the first two weeks, he allowed her to keep all of her clothes on. Then, he wanted her to take off her clothes so he could see her to help him get excited. The progression continued and he soon began touching her while she performed oral sex.

He made her kiss him on the lips. He would tell her he loved her and that he would always take care of her. He said she would always have a home with them (though he kept reminding her that she had nowhere else to go).

A month after he first began forcing her to have oral sex with him, he forced himself into her. He did this to her weekly at first. He had to make her stay up while everyone else went to bed and rape her in the living room. Rose and Stephanie still shared a room, and Jerry never would do anything with them at the same time, or to one while anyone else was in the room. Greg and Brian had their own rooms, and Linda was always too sound of a sleeper.

For the next six months to a year, he told Rose that he only had oral sex with Stephanie when Rose was on her period. He didn't like the way Rose performed oral sex because her buckteeth were uncomfortable to him. He had never tried to ejaculate in Rose's mouth, but would shove her head down until she gagged and choked.

He stopped having Rose perform oral sex on him after the first time he entered her, unless, he told her, Linda, Stephanie, and Rose were all on their periods at the same time. This happened only once or twice the whole six years Rose was there. After about six months, he said he had stopped with Stephanie altogether.

He told Rose, "If you don't have sex with me, I'll have to go back to having sex with Stephanie. Right now, I'm only having oral sex with her. That's all we do if she comes into my room. I don't feel right about having sex with Stephanie. She's my daughter and to have sex with her would be incest. That's a double sin. Since you're not my daughter, but my mistress, it's not as bad. Having sex with Stephanie would be totally different."

Rose didn't agree that having sex with her was less a sin than having sex with Stephanie. Sin was still sin. She didn't agree to be his mistress, either. This was not something she wanted to do. She was being raped!

19

The Bible agrees that having sex with a foster child is <u>not</u> less of a sin than having sex with a person's own child. In fact, Leviticus 19:33-34 says, "And if a stranger sojourn with thee in your land, ye shall not vex him. But the stranger that dwelleth with you shall be unto you as one born among you, and thou shalt love him as thyself." In other words, Jerry was supposed to treat Rose and Stephanie equally as daughters.

Since he was having sex with both, another verse comes into play. Leviticus 18:6 states, "None of you shall approach to any that is near of kin to him, to uncover their nakedness: I am the Lord." In other words, God will hold accountable and punish anyone who commits incest. Joined with Leviticus 19:33-34, this includes those who are related by birth, marriage, adoption, or even foster children who are staying with a family.

Rose felt she had to protect Stephanie, because of the love for her friend, though she still never agreed to have sex with him. Stephanie would never do anything to protect Rose, however, even when Jerry stopped having sex with her altogether, nor even when she married and left home. Even then, when there was no possibility of him going back to have sex with her if she reported him, she still let her "friend" suffer.

Rose would be forced to lie on the floor nude while Jerry did whatever he wanted to do. She always remained still, closing her eyes, trying not to think about what was happening to her. She didn't want to believe it. She would force her mind to think about other things. "I wish it wasn't me," she would think. "I wish I was a boy. I wish it was over."

When he finished, she put on her clothes as quickly as possible, said she had to go to the bathroom, and ran as fast as she could to it. She would sit on the toilet and cry as hard as she could.

He would go to his room and take a shower and tell her they would pray afterwards. He knelt down with her and asked God to forgive them and help them not to sin anymore, though **she** wasn't sinning. Only he was committing sin. God does not hold someone who is murdered accountable for being murdered. That person didn't commit the sin, the murderer did. Likewise, God counts a child or woman who is molested or raped innocent of the sin. They are the victims. God only holds accountable the molester or the rapist as guilty of committing the sin. No sin is accounted to the victim for the act done to them.

Jerry was, and is, the choir director of his church, the small Pentecostal-type church a few miles from his house. He would take them all to church regularly, often going to the altar to pray. Rose hoped he was praying for forgiveness and repenting (which means determining not to do something bad and, instead, to do something good. It literally means to make a change, a 180 degree change of direction), but he never stopped, and without repentance, there can be no forgiveness from God. This message is given by every prophet in the Bible—repent or face God's judgment. Jerry never repented.

Rose was getting very tired of him raping her, even though, he said, it was "only" once a week. Rose told him she would not do anything with him again, even if she didn't have anywhere to go and no matter how much he needed help.

"This is disgusting. It makes me feel disgusting. This is totally wrong. This is not Biblical," she told him, correctly. She started telling him Scriptures like Exodus 20:14, which reads, "Thou shalt not commit adultery;" and I Corinthians 6:18-20, which read, "Flee fornication [any sex outside of marriage]. Every sin that a man doeth is without the body; but he that committeth fornication sinneth against his own body. What? Know ye not that your body is the temple of the Holy Ghost which is in you, which ye have of God, and ye are not your own? For ye are bought with a price: therefore glorify God in your body, and in your spirit, which are God's."

"You filthy whore!" he shot back, interrupting her. "You're nothing but a two-bit whore. You're stupid and you'll never amount to anything. Don't quote Scripture to me. I know what the Bible says [Satan does, too, and like Jerry, he twists it for his own evil purposes to deceive people and justify his own actions]. I know what sin is and what sin is not, and I know God is justifying what we're doing because I need help in trying to meet my needs, and He understands that."

God, however, never condones or justifies sin. He condemns all sex outside of a marriage between a husband and wife as sin. Allah may justify sin for Muhammad, and other false gods, who are nothing more than fallen angels (demons), may justify sin for their cult members, but God Almighty never changes what He says is wrong for anybody—whether they be a preacher, pastor, Sunday School teacher, or anyone else. When He condemns something, he doesn't change His mind and allow it for just one person. He expects that person to repent and, if the need arises, to get professional counseling to stop his sinful actions.

"You are a whore," Jerry continued, "and you will have sex with me. That's all you are good for anyway. You'll never amount to anything. Besides, you know you have nowhere else to go, so you better just shut up and do what I say!"

The childcare organization and DFACS were supposed to contact Rose by now to make certain everything was going well. They never did. This only added to Rose's belief that she had nowhere else to go. Her aunt would not contact her until several years after she had been released from this hell. Rose felt truly alone and abandoned.

He progressed from raping her once a week to twice a week, then two to three times a week by her ninth grade year. This was when God had Chris pray for Rose though the two had never met, and wouldn't for six more years. Chris would pray for her nightly—for her protection and for God to comfort her—until he realized Rose was to be his wife. God knew Rose would need someone praying for her in the coming years. After a while, Jerry was raping her every other night, and when she got her own room, he did it nightly.

In her ninth grade year, Rose met a girl named Becky. Rose, Stephanie, and Becky would be good friends throughout high school, though Rose never told her what was being done to her. Becky would tell them about the football games that she attended. Jerry never allowed Rose to attend any of them.

The three would meet before school, during lunch, and after school (before the buses took them home), if they could. They would talk about boys—who they would like to date, who they wouldn't, and why.

They would play a game of following the guys around to see where they went—to which room they were going—before they had to go to their rooms for classes. They were pretending to be spies.

They never got to spend the night with each other. Jerry wouldn't let them talk on the phone. They did have a good time when they were together at school. All three took different kinds of classes, so they were never in the same class together.

By her tenth grade year, Jerry began to go to school occasionally to pick Rose up early. She knew that if her name was called over the intercom, it was he coming to take her home to rape her. He knew, as she did, that Linda would not be home for hours, and when the other children did get out of school, the bus ride for them was two hours long.

Rose and Stephanie were in the same grade together and, obviously, rode the same bus home. Stephanie never asked why Rose didn't ride the bus home or why didn't Jerry pick up all of the children early. She knew Rose was in for several hours of being raped, but still she said nothing. She just let Rose suffer. By her silence, she became just as guilty as Jerry of the rapes. She allowed the one who was supposedly her best friend suffer six long years of agony and she never tried to help end the suffering.

When Jerry would bring Rose home from school early, she often took off running in the yard, screaming she didn't want to have sex with him. He would yell back, "You whore! You know you're nothing but a whore! You're stupid and worthless. Even if I did let you date anybody [which he didn't], no man would want you because you've already had sex with me. No man wants to date a whore. You're free to go, but where would you go anyway?"

He would catch her and twist her arm behind her, forcing her back in the house. He would hit her a few times, usually busting her lip. He would push her down the hall and rape her despite her shouting no.

Linda never asked how Rose got the busted lips. She never brought it up, nor would she ask about Rose's puffy, red eyes from crying.

Jerry told Stephanie that if she ever told anybody, he would get in trouble and get sent to prison. He convinced her that Linda could not take care of all the children financially by herself. To Stephanie, keeping her father out of jail was more important than stopping her friend from being raped and beaten. She never did try to comfort Rose. She never said anything about what was going on, though Rose had confronted Stephanie about not warning her when Jerry first began to abuse Rose sexually. Stephanie never even apologized for not warning Rose nor coming to her aid, even years after Rose got out and the two met again. She told Rose she would never tell her mom or tell on her dad. She didn't want him to go to prison.

Jerry never would use any kind of protection, nor allow Rose to use any, not even the pill. She would pray every night, "Please, Lord, don't let me get pregnant. I don't want to be pregnant."

Rose's grades were dropping steadily the whole time she was with the D___s. This reinforced in her mind what Jerry told her about her being stupid. Her unpopularity and getting picked on by the other students because of her looks reinforced to her that nobody loved her and no man would want her.

Jerry wouldn't let her enroll in college prep classes, reminding her that she was "too stupid" to go to college. He would not allow her to get her driver's license, saying she was "too stupid" to drive herself anywhere. She might get in an accident and get killed. What he feared was that once she got a car or a license, she might leave and not return. He would lose his free sex, and away from there, she might get brave enough to report him.

School was Rose's only real refuge. She was glad when the bus came to pick her up and was glad that it took two hours to get back home. By then, Linda would be home, and he wouldn't touch her until that night.

On Saturdays, Linda would go shopping in Royston and be gone for several hours. She would always ask who wanted to go with her. Rose really wanted to go, to get away from Jerry, but he always instructed her ahead of time that she had better not go. She would always tell Linda no, her heart breaking inside. Linda would take everyone else, leaving Rose to fend for herself with Jerry.

As usual, he would take off his clothes and make her take off hers. He would lay her on the bed and have sex with her. She would never respond to him in any way. She would wish to herself that she were free from her prison and that he would hurry up so she could get away from him. If she resisted in any way, he would call her names, hit her, and if need be, chase her through the house, knocking her down and raping her anyway.

If she dared to resist him at night, when everyone else was asleep, he would give her an evil look. That look made her blood freeze. She sincerely thought he was going to murder her if she made any more noise or refused him further.

He often told Rose that Linda no longer satisfied him, that she was too loose because of having three children. He complained that she wouldn't touch him and that once she was asleep, he couldn't hope to have sex with her that night because she slept too hard. He said she didn't do anything for him in bed, and felt like a "wet noodle" anyway. He would tell Rose he needed someone who was loving, caring, and warm, and someone who would have sex with him.

He never tried to get Rose excited before entering her. She was so repulsed by this troll she couldn't have gotten turned on by him anyway, but he never tried. He was only concerned about himself. She never acted loving or caring to him. He would just force himself into her regardless of how she acted, causing her to bleed profusely in the early years. He would sometimes use lubricants to make it easier to enter her, but that was rare. Nine out of ten times, he showed her his pornographic material, but still she remained dry and unexcited. He made her watch him masturbate using them once or twice.

He would not allow her to date. He would tell her he loved her and he wanted her to be his mistress always. He insisted he would always take care of her. He would never allow her to invite friends over or go to anyone else's house. She couldn't call anyone, and if anyone called her, he would interrogate her as to the identity of the caller, the purpose for the call, and what was said.

Jerry allowed Stephanie to date and to attend parties if she so desired, but not Rose. Rose only got to go anywhere if she sent a request to the child-care organization and they got her the things she needed for her to go.

At the end of her second year with the D___s, Rose was taken for a vacation to the main campus of the child-care organization to visit Mike and Denise, the former directors of the relief home. Jerry and Linda went, too, partly to visit their "friends," Mike and Denise, but in Jerry's case, mostly to make sure Rose didn't report him or escape from his clutches. He never touched her the whole time they were there, but warned her she had better not say anything or he would "get her."

This was the first contact the child-care organization had had with Rose since she had been with the D___s. They were supposed to contact and visit her regularly, but for two years, she had heard nothing from them until she went to the main campus. Mike and Denise had transferred from the relief shelter to the main campus because there was more help at the main campus and they could have more time for their family. The "official" reason for Rose's visit thus became an opportunity for Jerry and Linda to visit their old friends since they had moved away from Dewey Rose, where the relief shelter and the D___'s house were.

Jerry told Rose that he and Linda were her legal guardians now and if she said anything to try to get the organization to move her elsewhere, she would be the one suffering for it. He told her that the organization had no real authority over her anymore anyway. Also, she would be responsible for tearing up his family (though he would have been the only one responsible). She already had a low self-esteem and felt dirty, guilty, and ashamed, so he took advantage of this.

"I'll just find someone else anyway," he threatened. "The agency has nowhere to move you. They haven't contacted you in two years. There is nowhere else for you to go. We're your legal guardians now, so you can't do anything, anyway. Who would take in a teenager who is almost an adult and has problems anyway?" Rose was sixteen by this time. She was convinced that saying something would accomplish nothing but getting herself in trouble.

Rose was thankful for the time away from being raped. She was able to go swimming and play—to be a kid again, until it was time to go back to Dewey Rose. Mike and Denise did not find out that anything was happening and Rose said nothing. When they returned to Dewey Rose, the rapings resumed as usual.

While still at the main campus, Rose asked her caseworker if she could go see her mom, whom Rose had not seen since her mom had been put into a mental institution. She was now living in a group home for people suffering from mental illness instead of living in the institution. The group home was located in Douglasville.

Rose's caseworker said she would set up a place for Rose to stay in Douglasville with a caseworker for DFACS there. That caseworker found Paul and Glennie Tolbert. Rose would stay with them when she would go visit her mom for one week during Christmas holidays and one week during the summers. She would catch a Gray Hound bus either in Athens or Elberton to go to Douglasville for those trips for the next few years. Linda would take her to the bus station. Jerry never would.

Rose would spend the night with them, and they would take her to spend the days with her mom. On Sundays, they would pick up Rose's mom and they would all go to Soul's Arbor, the church founded and pastored by Glennie's son, Glen. Rose was always thankful for those times, partly because she would get a break from Jerry, partly because she could see her mom, and partly because she grew spiritually under Pastor Glen's guidance.

She would wish she could stay with the Tolberts, but she told them nothing of the hell she was enduring. They were strict, but loving. Paul and Glennie were an elderly couple who could have retired, but always had too much energy to do so. Even today, they still keep foster children. They lay down the rules and expect them to be obeyed. Every foster child knows to obey, but all of the ones that the Tolberts have kept know that the Tolberts genuinely love each of them, no matter how long or short their stay is.

Paul was a widower with his own children and Glennie a widow with hers as well. They had married but were too old by then to have any children together. All of their children were already grown, some with children of their own.

Glennie was the talkative one. She wouldn't gossip, for gossip is unbiblical and condemned by God, but still she was the center of the information chain for her whole family down to the grandchildren. She was also a source for information for the church. She would not tell secrets. Most of the conversations would be about who had their baby and its statistics, important events to remember, birthdays and anniversaries and the like.

She made most of the decisions for the house and handled most of the discipline. Paul would rarely say a word to anyone. His mere presence made children behave. If a look became necessary, children would act like angels. There would seldom be a third step. He rarely even smiled. If he disagreed with Glennie, he would tell her and she would comply with his wishes—which is probably why he let her run most things.

If he opened his mouth to say anything, even adults would get quiet and listen to what he had to say. He was feared, loved, and revered all at the same time by everyone. He was a constant in the lives of every foster child that stayed with them, and they loved him for it.

He would pretend like he was spanking them, they giggling the whole time, and then he would tickle them until they were hysterical. He would give each one a hug and a kiss on the cheek before bedtime, then watch TV as Glennie escorted them all to bed. Every child and many adults called them Grandmother and Paw-paw, whether they were related to the Tolberts or not.

While staying with the Tolberts on these trips, Rose met a guy named Bill J. He had his own Christian band. He was singing at Soul's Arbor the Sunday of Rose's first trip to see her mom. This trip occurred the Christmas after Rose and the D___s went to the main campus to meet Mike and Denise. Rose could sense the Spirit of God all around him. "I want what he's got," she told herself. She sensed peace and love around him.

Rose thought she was attracted to him physically, but says now that she realizes she was attracted to him spiritually. She didn't know anyone back where she lived upon whom she could sense the presence of God. She wanted to feel God's presence all the time, especially while she was suffering with the D___s.

After the service, she talked to him and told him where she was living but that she had to leave and go back soon. She wanted to know if he would write to her, to which he agreed. They wrote to each other on a regular basis from then until her senior year of high school. He had moved away by then to Nebraska.

In those letters, Rose never told him what was happening to her. She was afraid that if anyone found out what was happening to her, they wouldn't want to date her or have anything to do with her. She rarely even mentioned herself, because she was so ashamed of herself. They mostly talked about him and what he was doing.

CHAPTER FIVE

By the third year, Rose was under mounting depression. She was hard on herself, blaming herself. After each sexual encounter with Jerry, she spent more time in the bathroom crying.

She took walks most afternoons. There, she would talk to God. "Lord, I just want out. Just let me out, but don't let me get pregnant."

Jerry was having sex with her every other day. He still did not try to get her excited before entering her. No matter how much she hurt, he didn't care. He never asked if he was hurting her physically or emotionally. He never asked what she felt. He was only concerned with getting that next orgasm.

Before her third year, Rose would quickly get dressed and run to the bathroom afterwards, trying unsuccessfully to cleanse herself by showering of the sense of filth she felt. After they had both showered, he would read Scriptures with her and pray, not realizing that God does not listen to unrepentant prayers. By the third year, he had quit praying for deliverance and was having sex with her every other day. She was now seventeen and a sophomore in Hart County High School in Hartwell. She would still tell him no. She still didn't want to have sex with him.

"You know I control this family, and I control you," he would reply. Then he would repeat what he had been saying for three years—that she was stupid, a whore, she had nowhere else to go, and that no man would ever want her anyway. "You'll never amount to anything," he insisted.

He only allowed her to go anywhere while she was on her period, and that was only with Linda to the store. Sometimes he allowed Stephanie to take her out, but rarely.

Sometimes Linda would go out and leave the boys at home, too. During these times, Jerry would make Rose go in his room and he would tell the boys, who were around ten and eleven years old, not to come in there. They saw Rose go in, but at that age, it was doubtful whether they knew what was going on. They never said anything to Linda about it and never came into the room while Rose was being raped.

At this time, he decided Rose and Stephanie needed separate rooms. He told Linda it was because Rose and Stephanie were old enough to need their own rooms. Linda agreed. What Jerry really wanted was to be able to have a private room in which to rape Rose. As often as he was having sex with Rose, the living room just wasn't safe enough anymore.

The boys, who had had separate rooms, were made to share the front bedroom, which had been the girl's room, and were given bunk beds. Stephanie was given the back bedroom, and Rose was given the middle room. Now Jerry could sneak in her room at night, lock the door, and rape her every night and hopefully, to him—not Rose—not get caught.

He would not warn Rose that he would be coming in that night. The house would be dark and everyone asleep. Rose would be startled awake by Jerry climbing into her bed stark naked and trying to pull her clothes off. If she tried to resist, or hold her clothing, he would overpower her and yank her clothes off anyway. If she said no, she wouldn't have sex with him, he would reply, "Oh, yes you will, and you better be quiet before you wake everyone else up and get us in trouble." Then he would rape her as he always did.

Rose felt horrible about herself. "Lord, please don't come back yet," she would pray. She was afraid that if the Lord Jesus did return to collect his believers and take them to heaven with him, in what Christians call the Rapture, then she would be left behind. She thought that even though she had accepted Jesus as her Lord and Savior and had never willingly had sex with Jerry, her filthiness from being raped repeatedly for the past three years would cause God to reject her. She did not realize that God did not blame her for what had been done to her, but that He had been with her all this time, strengthening her.

He promises that He will never leave or forsake anyone who truly trusts Him as Lord and Savior. He also promises that the sins we commit in secret will be shown openly. He kept both of these promises.

Jerry would sometimes take them to revival meetings. At one of these, Rose prayed to be filled and baptized with the Holy Spirit. The Holy Spirit is the third person of the Trinity, God himself. It is the Holy Spirit who draws us to Jesus and lives in our hearts after we accept Jesus as Savior and Lord. When we yield to His leading, He gives us the strength and ability to live the Christian life, which we cannot do on our own. God the Father promises to give the Holy Spirit to any who ask. This was what Rose did, and she received the Holy Spirit's fullness just as the 120 disciples had on the Day of Pentecost, recorded in Acts 2.

Before this time, Rose had been unable to sense the Lord's presence with her, though he had been there all along. This revival meeting occurred a month after Rose got her own room. After being filled with the Holy Spirit, she began feeling the presence of the Lord with her.

She felt depressed, dirty, and ashamed. She was sad constantly. Others would comment that she was very sweet and humble, but she wondered if it was just her sadness and shame showing through. She had no respect for herself. She didn't think she was pretty, and thought that no boy was interested in her. She thought she couldn't get a boyfriend if she tried, so she didn't try. She would never flirt. She felt dirty and shameful and thought all she could do was satisfy Jerry. That is what Jerry was telling her.

"You'll never be able to satisfy a man, and nobody would want you anyway," he would tell her, increasing her hopelessness. Even after she was wed years later, she was still afraid that she couldn't satisfy her husband sexually.

Rose began to read her Bible daily and pray. She would go for a lot of walks, praying as she walked. It was on these walks that she would feel God's presence the most. He would wrap her in love and assure her that He would deliver her. "Until then," He would reassure her, "I'm still with you always. You are never alone, even when you can't sense My presence."

Once inside the house, she seldom felt His presence. The Satanic presence filling that home was too strong for her. She couldn't sense anything else.

On her walks, she would walk down the road. Jerry didn't worry about her running away. They were so far out in the country that there weren't any close neighbors to whom she could run.

Shortly, Rose would come to a dirt road that went off to the left. A little way down this dirt road, she would go down a dirt path to a pond. This was her sanctuary, the place where she could get alone with God.

Rose would climb a tree by the pond and watch the fish swim and the frogs hop and swim around. Nobody ever came down there while she was there. Sometimes, after Jerry raped her, she would run to the bathroom to cry and pray, and she would feel the Lord's comforting presence with her a little. At the pond, though, when she was out of that house and alone with God, she could feel the presence of God all around her, overwhelming her with His love.

These walks helped her to endure until God delivered her out of her bondage as He had the ancient Israelites who were slaves in Egypt and the blacks who were slaves in this country. She would thank Him for the grass, the trees, the flowers, even the dirt. She would thank Him for the world itself.

"You created everything so beautiful," she would say, amazed at the wonders of God's creation. "And You created it just for us. And You created us for Yourself. Thank You." She would feel His presence so strongly that it was as if He was sitting there beside her, listening, and she could almost reach out and touch Him. "It was as if He were sitting there listening to me and whatever I had to say," she would testify years later. This was how she spent most of her Saturdays.

"Thank You for being with me, Lord. I want out. Please help me get out of here," she would pray. She tried to go to church more often with friends. Jerry relaxed for a little time, allowing her to go to church with friends, but nowhere else.

About this time, Jerry was going to church less and less often, but still remained the choir director. He told his family he wasn't getting fed spiritually at his church, so they could all try different churches. It is no wonder he wasn't hearing from God at this time, with what he was doing to Rose. It was because of this, though, that he allowed Rose to go with friends to other churches. He would soon stop going to church at all, and cease praying with Rose after raping her.

Rose met a friend named Laura Richardson and went to her church a few times. Laura's pastor knew Christian recording artist Mylon LeFevre. He asked Mylon to come to Hartwell and give a concert, and talked the principal into letting them use the gym at the high school after school hours for a free concert at the end of their tenth grade year.

Jerry allowed Rose to go to the concert. Rose went forward to talk to Mylon after the concert. She was so tired of the situation, she was finally willing to tell someone and get help. She told him what Jerry had been doing to her. He said, "I've got to get you some help." Mylon talked to the pastor, then he and the pastor confronted Jerry.

Jerry agreed that if they wouldn't report him, he and Rose would go to counseling. He went a few times, then stopped. He was so far away from God, no amount of counseling would help without repentance, though. He didn't rape Rose for a few months, hoping everything would blow over and be forgotten. It was.

A few days after the concert, Tony and Denitra, Linda's cousins, came to the area to do a kid's crusade with singing, dancing, tumbling, acting, and prayer. The church, of which Jerry had been choir director, sponsored the crusade. They asked Rose to play a part in it, which she did. They were so impressed with her performance that they asked her to travel with them. To aid the appearance that he was getting better, Jerry allowed her to go for a few weeks. This happened during the summer between her tenth and eleventh grade years.

She traveled with them to several places, glad to be away from Jerry. She had a lot of fun, and enjoyed telling children about Jesus. During this time, Tony and Denitra took Rose to their home church. She doesn't know what city or state it was in. The pastor's name was David. His son, David, Jr., was very nice to Rose. He would tell her she looked nice and had a pretty complexion. He said he could tell she had a very sweet spirit about her and that she was very humble. He said she seemed like a good Christian woman and he could tell God was with her. "You'll have a good life," he told her.

Rose blushed. No guy had ever been nice to her before like this. "If he would have asked me to marry him right then, I'd have done it in a heartbeat," she would confess years later. She never saw him again, though, after that day.

Before the service started, he showed her around the church. He talked about the church and his father's ministry. At the altar call after the service, Rose went forward for prayer. It was then that God started the healing process in her spirit.

After two months of leaving Rose alone, Jerry came into her room one night telling her he couldn't take it anymore. "God shouldn't have made you so attractive and wonderful and so appealing sexually," he told her. This is what most people do—they neither take responsibility for their actions, nor do they determine to change things. Instead, they blame God, their parents, or society for their wrong acts and for the things that happen to them. Jerry resumed raping her every other night as if nothing had happened to stop them.

"If you tell anyone else, you'll be seriously in trouble. I'll have you locked up because you're an equal partner in this. You're willing to do it and we have an equal partnership. You're just as guilty as I am for having sex with me. If I get in trouble, so will you," he threatened her the very next day.

All of this was a lie. She had **never** been willing, and beside that, she was under age and he would be considered guilty of statutory rape—having sex with a minor.

She turned eighteen her junior year. She was legally an adult now, so he told her, "You're an adult now, so if you say anything to anybody, you'll get in trouble, too. You'll go to jail for getting me in trouble because you're just as guilty as I am." Again, this was a lie. She was never willing to have sex with him.

Rose was praying more frequently, asking God to get her out of her situation. Consequently, she resisted Jerry more. He became increasingly violent in response. He would hit her and call her names more. The way he looked at Rose got more evil. His psychological state got worse and worse.

Some diseases, both physical and mental, are a result of natural causes. Some, however, result from demonic attacks on persons, sometimes to the point of controlling a person's actions, though the person can still get freedom through prayer and obedience to God and seeking help from a knowledgeable Christian who understands spiritual warfare.

Many Christians make the mistake of seeing all sickness and mental illness as an attack from Satan and his demons. Many secular doctors and psychiatrists make the opposite and equally damaging assumption that everything can be explained by natural causes. The best way of seeing sickness and mental illness is that it can be either all natural, all demonic, or some of both. The best course of action is to seek first a natural cause. If everything fails, and no source can be discovered for an illness, mental or physical, then look for spiritual answers.

As a Christian, why do I say look for the physical first? The reason is that physical answers are less traumatic than telling a person at the onset that they have demons. When sicknesses cannot be explained by natural causes, the persons are more receptive to spiritual answers than they may have been before. Being more receptive, then, it will be easier to receive spiritual healing and help.

When a person is under demonic control, it is usually easily visible on the face, especially in the eyes. This was the case with King Saul when he would attack David in the Old Testament. Rose says she could tell when Jerry wanted to have sex with her. His eyes would literally change and an evil presence would come about him. His personality would change, too.

31

"It was terrifying and horrible and it would give me the creeps every time. Just to look at him would just scare me," Rose reports. "He had such an evil expression. It was just pure evil—just horrible."

A born again Christian who is faithful has no need to worry about demons entering him or her and controlling his or her actions. A Christian who habitually yields to sin rather than God opens himself up for demonic activity as much as an unbeliever. This is what Jesus meant when he said, "Give no place to the devil," and in Him, Jesus, there was no such place.

Many Christians would object to this, saying that a Christian has God living inside of him. They often quote the Scripture that says our bodies are the temples of the Holy Spirit. Their rationale is that God and Satan can't be in the same place at the same time. The book of Job shows us, however, that Satan does come into God's presence, and regularly.

The ancient Jews used this same line of reasoning to convince themselves that if they had the Ark of the Covenant, then located in Shiloh, they could not be defeated because of God's presence. Because of their sins, however, God allowed Israel to be defeated, the Ark taken by enemies, Shiloh plundered, and even the priest, Eli, fell dead when hearing about it.

The Israelites used this same rationale later on, when the Ark of the Covenant was in Jerusalem in the temple. Again, because of habitual sins, the prophet Ezekiel said that the presence of God had left the temple, a thing heretical to them. They continued unrepentant until Nebuchadnezzar, king of Babylon, sacked Jerusalem and emptied the land of almost all Hebrew inhabitants.

Jeremiah, the prophet, said they should submit to Nebuchadnezzar because this was a punishment from God for their sinful acts. He said it would be easier for them just to submit—they'd suffer less that way—and that they'd be back in seventy years anyway. The Israelites accused him of treason and had him thrown into a dungeon.

Years later, the Jewish leaders killed the Messiah as Isaiah, hundreds of years earlier, had prophesied that they would. This is not said because of any assumed Christian-Jewish hatred. Jesus was a Jew, the disciples and apostles were Jews. The early converts were all Jews. As Christians, we, the authors, believe that the Jews are still God's chosen people and that He's not through with them. What we are saying is that at the time of Jesus, the Jewish leaders were habitually sinning, as were many of the people. They used the same rationale as before—God would never allow Israel to be defeated because of the temple, which symbolized His presence—not willing to repent of their actions. They even rebelled against Roman rule and were crushed so thoroughly that from A.D. 70 to the 20th century, there was no nation of Israel.

The issue, then, is not whether God and Satan can be in the same person or place, but whether God will continue to protect a person from Satanic invasion if that person habitually commits the same sin unrepentantly. Even though such a person may claim to be faithfully serving God, in reality, just like the judge Samson, who committed habitual unrepentant sin, they "know not that the Spirit of God has left" them, leaving them wide open for Satan.

When the evil presence would come on Jerry, Rose would say, "Jerry, why don't we just go pray or something like that instead of trying to do something like this," meaning sex.

"Oh, I know what I'm doing," he would answer. "I know God is approving of what I'm doing. He knows I'm not trying to do it, but I have to do it because Linda is not satisfying me." He would say anything to justify his actions.

"Don't quote me the Bible," he would state, forcibly. "I know what it says. I've been reading the Bible a long time. I've been a Christian a long time." Before this time, he had often listened to records of old-time gospel singing and hymns. Now, he no longer did. A person who chooses to reject God's leading and continue in sin is angry when confronted by the Word of God and the conviction of the Holy Spirit, which conviction reminds a person much like a nagging conscience that that person needs to repent and return to God.

After a while, though, God will stop convicting a person of sin. Romans 1 says that in such a case, God "gives them up to a reprobate mind." The context of Romans 1 is talking about homosexuals who refuse to repent even when told their actions are wrong in the sight of God. They are described as not just continuing in sin, but turning violent in opposition to God and His Word—much like current organizations such as Act-Up.

Romans 1 applies to everyone who rejects the conviction of God. This was the case with Jerry. He was violently opposed to God and His Word, especially when it was saying that what Jerry was doing was wrong.

At this time, Jerry used a Polaroid camera and took nude pictures of Rose when nobody was around. His sinful actions were getting worse and increasing in frequency. He had picked Rose up from school and made her undress in his bedroom. He made her pose for him in different ways. He didn't force her to have sex that day. He told her he wanted to put those pictures with his magazines so that he would have something of her to look at. This didn't make Rose feel sexy. She couldn't understand why he wanted pictures of her, though he often told her she was sexy and had a good body. This made Rose feel gross, ashamed, and embarrassed. She hopes that he has destroyed them since then, but doesn't know if he did. This was the only time he took pictures of her.

Jerry was also treating his children worse. "He got very mean to them. He got really horrible with his kids the last two years I was there," Rose recalls. Greg, the peacemaker, always did whatever his father asked, without question. Brian hated Jerry, even telling him so a couple of times. He wouldn't do what Jerry told him to do.

Unlike Greg, Brian had no interest in going to fix the tractor and doing other things that would get the boys outside so Jerry could rape Rose. He wanted to play and watch cartoons. Consequently, Jerry would often hit Brian.

"One time," Rose remembers, "we were all sitting at the table. Jerry said, 'Son, I hate to do this.' He grabbed Brian's shirt and started banging his head against the back of the chair. He yanked him out of the chair and started hitting him. Then he picked him up and threw him against the wall.

"'Now that is tough love,' Jerry told him. 'And I want you to know, I'm the head of this household and you do not talk to me like that!'

"He didn't get hard on Stephanie. She was his little girl and she did whatever he said, too," Rose recalls. "His whole personality changed, though. He became more evil all the time."

"I don't know how Jerry and Linda's relationship was at this time," Rose admits. "I could tell it was more strained. She would always do everything he asked, though. She fixed him coffee, fixed him supper, waited on him hand and foot. She did everything for that man. She washed his clothes, ironed them, and folded them. She always kept a neat, clean house. She fixed him all kinds of desserts. She tried to please him in every way she could, but the harder she tried, the more he seemed to ignore her. It seemed like he didn't appreciate her at all. It was just sad."

"I'll never, ever have a relationship like that with my husband," Rose promised herself. "Me and my husband's relationship will always be loving and always be a mutual agreement on stuff; and I'll always submit unto him as a wife, but I won't be treated like she is being treated."

"Lord, please send me a good, godly husband—a husband who would never, ever do anything like that. Let him be one who will love me and accept me for who I am and the way I am—not the way anyone else wants me to be, but who I am—the real me."

During her eleventh grade year, another foster child came to live with the D___s. He had been a twin. At age 5, his mother threw his brother out of a four-story window, killing him. He escaped while she was doing this to his brother, but he saw his twin die. Jerry used even this innocent child as leverage to keep Rose quiet.

"If you say anything to anybody, they'll take him away, too. You know he doesn't have anywhere else to go. He doesn't need the trauma of losing another home. You'd be hurting him, too," Jerry would say.

"If you don't stay, we can't keep [the other foster child]. You would be destroying his life as well as yours. He loves us, trusts us, and needs us. You shouldn't mess up his life by trying to leave." Rose couldn't bear the thought of causing anyone or anything pain, especially this little boy who had already been through so much.

Jerry allowed Rose and Stephanie to get a job the summer between their eleventh and twelfth grade years at a local seafood restaurant, the Swamp Guinea [sic?]. They were both waitresses, making pretty good money, especially during local high school football games, Georgia-Clemson games, and if anyone came in drunk.

They saved up enough money to buy a car together—a tiny, lime-green Ford Festiva. He wouldn't let Rose drive it. She would sometimes back it up and down the driveway, but nowhere else. Jerry allowed Stephanie to get her license, but not Rose. His "whore" could never be allowed the same privileges as his daughter. Stephanie was allowed to live a pretty normal teenage life, but not Rose.

Rosalee & T. Christopher Jarrell

CHAPTER SIX

Rose's senior year was her worst. Jerry would have sex with her at least once a day, sometimes several times, if he could get away with it. Her period was her only safe time. She was nineteen now. He knew she would be graduating soon, so he was getting worse. She no longer prayed not to get pregnant. "Lord, I don't care how you get me out of here, just get me out!" she prayed instead.

One night half way through her senior year, after Jerry had raped her, Rose had gone into the bathroom to cry and pray. She was still crying when she went back to bed. "Lord, just let me out. Show me that you are going to let me out," she prayed.

During her sleep, the Lord gave her two dreams. One was about a dark, black cloud. It hovered over the school bus while Rose rode it. It hovered over school, and followed her home. Linda took Rose somewhere in her silver car, and it followed then, too. Rose then saw a man's hand in the sky pushing the black cloud away. The sky was clear and blue and pretty. "Thank you, Lord, for the silver lining in the midst of the storm," Rose prayed.

The second dream was of Rose walking down a long, dirt road. There would be darkness, then a ray of sunshine, more darkness, and another ray of sunshine. Rose was coming to a curve in the road. A voice told her, "The sunshine is just around the curve. Just keep walking."

Rose felt like she had left her body and her spirit was floating up onto the ceiling. This was not a new-age out-of-body experience, which is a counterfeit of what God sometimes does. Satan, who has inspired the New Age movement, is no originator, but only a counterfeiter. He tries to copy what God does with the purpose of turning people away from God and the truth.

"There were angels all around my body," Rose reports. "It was such a lovely experience. But, then I looked down and saw my body. What am I doing up here?" she asked. She returned to her body, but could still feel the angels around her.

"Thank you, Lord, for those angels," she prayed. "I don't care how you let me out, just let me out."

Rose reports that she could feel God with her more and more. "I knew He knew what was going on. I knew He cared about me and He loved me, and that He would take care of it all. I just knew it after that," Rose recalls. She says that this made it more bearable because she knew it would end.

One Saturday, around this time, Linda went to the store as she usually did on Saturdays. Again, Jerry made Rose stay home. Usually, Linda would take the other children and go pick up her mom. She would take her to the beauty parlor and let her get her hair done, and she would go shopping with the children. This gave Jerry several hours to rape Rose.

This Saturday, that demonic look came over Jerry's face. "You know what I want to do," he said. He took her to the bedroom. "You know I love you," he said.

"Yeah, right!" she thought to herself.

"I care for you. I'll treat you right. If it wasn't for us, you wouldn't have a place to stay, anyway. You'd be living out in the street."

Jerry closed his bedroom door like he always did. He put an end table in front of it because the lock was broken. He made Rose strip herself, and he took off his clothes, too. Rose estimates that halfway through this act of sex, Linda came home early.

Rose doesn't know if he was making noise, but Linda came and banged on the door, demanding to know what they were doing. At first, she couldn't open the door because of the table, but did finally force it open. She saw them lying there, in the act.

"What do you think you're doing?" she shouted, a look of complete shock on her face.

"Oh I didn't mean to. This was a one-time thing," he lied. "Rose, get up and get dressed. I'll handle this. Go in yonder."

Rose did as she was told. She was too ashamed to look at Linda in the eye. She walked past her with her head down. They closed the door, and Rose doesn't know what was said. She was even more ashamed than usual, now that Linda knew. Linda never apologized for Jerry's actions; never accused Rose of anything. She never even talked to Rose about what had happened or for how long it had been going on.

Linda didn't cry. She didn't treat Rose any differently than before. She wasn't mean to Rose, but she was more careful after that about leaving Rose alone with Jerry. For the next few weeks, she wouldn't let Rose stay home alone with Jerry, but Jerry sneaked around and had sex with Rose at night anyway. After about three weeks, Linda foolishly started letting Rose stay home alone with Jerry as if nothing had happened.

Linda did try to get Jerry to go to bed with her more and not to stay up with Rose. She wore her makeup more often, and bought herself some lingerie. She bought douche and began using it.

"We're having sex more often," she told Rose, "so I hope that helps." She didn't call the childcare organization or tell anyone, though.

Jerry had not stopped having sex with Rose, but he had gotten more cautious. Because of Linda's stupidity for trusting her husband, who had already proven himself to be untrustworthy, things resumed just as if they had not gotten caught. He still made Rose stay up at night so he could rape her, still occasionally picked her up from school early, and still made her stay home on Saturdays while Linda went to the store, all so he could rape Rose.

With this being their Senior year, Stephanie, Becky, and Rose would talk about where they wanted to go to college. Stephanie wanted to go to cosmetology school. Rose and Becky wanted to go to Emmanuel College, a small Christian school just outside of Royston. The two didn't know what they wanted to do for the rest of their lives, or even what major they wanted to take.

The time for the senior prom was fast approaching. Rose, Becky, and Stephanie all wanted to go. Stephanie begged Jerry to allow Rose to go because it would be the last time all three would be together. After many attempts by Stephanie, and a little intervention by Linda, Jerry finally agreed, but he would not buy Rose a dress or pay for the trip. Rose asked the childcare organization to help, and they paid for everything she needed.

Stephanie drove their little Ford Festiva. None of the three had dates. They didn't dance the whole time. They only sat at a table and talked and watched. Nobody asked them to dance. After two or three hours of sitting by themselves, they left and ate pizza. They spent the rest of the evening talking.

Stephanie and Rose returned home after everyone else was in bed. Thankfully, Jerry didn't wake up and come into her room that night, so she had a whole day to enjoy.

Soon afterwards, their car stopped working and would never be repaired. All the CV joints went out at the same time, and since repairs would cost more than the car itself, they just left it in the yard.

Jerry wouldn't pay for the things Rose needed for graduation, either. The child-care organization paid for this, too. Rose bought her Senior Class ring with the money she had saved from working.

After graduation, Stephanie got another car so she could go to college. Jerry had made Rose help pay for gas and everything on their first car, though he wouldn't let her drive it. Now, he forced Rose to help Stephanie pay for a car so Stephanie could go to college. "It made me so mad!" Rose reports. "He wouldn't let me use it, but made me pay for the stupid thing!" Stephanie was still planning to attend cosmetology school.

"You're too stupid to go to college," Jerry would tell Rose. "You don't need college. You're too stupid even to be accepted into one. You don't even have your driver's license, anyway." He had never taught her to drive, nor would he allow anyone else to teach her. He wouldn't even allow Rose to apply to any colleges.

"She just doesn't have what it takes to do well in college," he would say if Linda were present. He wouldn't call Rose stupid in front of Linda.

Rose went to work with Linda at a local sewing factory, called Rogin's, located in Bowman. By the time Rose turned twenty that November, she knew that she was pregnant. She had already missed two or more periods. She didn't want to admit it, though, hoping her periods would resume any day.

During the summer, Rose went to see her Mom, who was now living in Cedartown. Rose already knew she was pregnant before she left to go visit her mother. She had not told Jerry, and she had not been to the doctor to confirm it, but she had already missed her August period.

Rose's mother was finally living on her own again, so Rose just stayed with her, but Rose didn't tell her mom anything. Rose wasn't certain her mother would understand, or if she did, it might cause her to get worse again, resulting in a return to a mental institution. Rose stayed with her mom the whole time, seeing no one.

When Rose returned to Dewey Rose, she met another guy named Bill, a different one than Bill J., whom she had met years earlier. Jerry allowed her to go on a date with him, which shocked Rose. On their first date, he took her to dinner and a movie, then back home.

Later, he told Rose that he had a friend who wasn't seeing anybody and wondered if Stephanie would go out with him. Bill and Rose asked Stephanie and she said she would go. The three of them asked Jerry if they could all go out on a double date for Halloween. He agreed to this date as well.

Stephanie's date would later become her husband. They four drove around together, looking at the decorations. They separated and Bill took Rose home. She told him she couldn't see him anymore, not giving him an explanation, but telling him not to call again.

They had never had sex—they didn't even know each other very well, but she knew Jerry would try to blame the baby on him if the relationship continued. She couldn't let Jerry off scott free after all the years of torture he'd put her through— six long, tearful years. Jerry had gotten her pregnant, not Bill or anyone else.

She really couldn't bear the thought of an innocent person getting stuck with the responsibility for caring for her and her baby. She knew girls who slept around with many guys and got pregnant. They would seduce morally upright guys whom they knew would feel guilty and take the responsibility to care for them and their babies, knowing full well these guys were not the fathers. Rose was not that kind of girl. She had never willingly had sex with anyone, and she could not let someone else be held responsible for Jerry's evil actions.

Rose also met a guy named Ed. His mother worked at Rogin's with Rose. He would come and visit his mother at work. This was how he met Rose. They never dated. He would come over to the D___'s house and sit with Rose on the front porch in the swing. They talked about work and other small talk. They would often sit silently, just swinging. He said he just wanted Rose to know that he was her friend. This helped Rose to see that guys might be interested in her in a non-sexual way.

The very next day after the second date with Bill, in which she ended the relationship, Rose told Jerry she thought that she was pregnant and that she had missed a couple of periods.

"What are we going to say?" Jerry asked.

"I don't know, but I don't want to blame it on Bill. Me and Bill never did do anything. He is not the father. I don't want him being forced to marry me," she said. She knew that this was what Jerry would try to do, if she allowed it. She knew she didn't want it, and neither did God.

"Give the child up for adoption," God told Rose during this conversation. She has no doubts that God wanted her to give the baby up for adoption.

"I'll think of something," Jerry assured her. "Don't worry about it. I'll think of something to tell her," meaning Linda.

He told Linda that while Rose was visiting her mom in Cedartown that summer, someone had gotten her drunk or high and had raped her. Rose had spent all her time with her mom, and she had never had alcohol or drugs in her life. Rose didn't contradict him, though.

Linda set up a doctor's appointment and he confirmed that Rose was pregnant. He asked Rose what she wanted to do. She replied she didn't know what she wanted to do with the baby.

She knew she didn't want to have an abortion. She didn't believe in abortion. She knew that murdering the baby would not make what Jerry had done right. It wasn't the baby's fault. The baby couldn't help the circumstances under which he was conceived.

Murdering the baby wouldn't help her forget the six years of repeated rape that Jerry had put her through. She would have the innocent blood of the baby on her hands, and she knew she couldn't live with that. She was the victim in the case of rape. If she had the baby aborted, she would have been guilty of paying to have a licensed assassin kill her baby. Even though the Supreme Court would approve, God and her conscience would not.

The church that they had been attending accepted Rose (and her pregnancy). Nobody anywhere asked her about her pregnancy or the baby. The church accepted her for the way she was. They showered her with love, just as churches should do. They didn't care about the circumstances of her pregnancy. They didn't ask about it, and Rose didn't offer any explanations. They just loved her regardless of her situation.

Even though nobody asked Rose how she got pregnant, she felt so dirty and ashamed that she felt she didn't even belong in her church. "I felt so ashamed of myself because I was pregnant and didn't have a boyfriend. I couldn't get married. I was having somebody else's baby out of wedlock, and he was married. It was just a bad situation. It was horrible. But, God was with me."

Everyone at Rogin's also knew that she was pregnant. Ed also knew. He still came around, sat on the porch with her, and talked. He continued to be her friend. "I'm here if you want to talk to somebody," he said.

Rose told Linda and Jerry that she wanted to put the baby up for adoption even though she didn't know how to go about it. She assured them that this was what she desired. They said she could keep it if she wanted to keep it. She told them no, she wanted to give the baby up for adoption.

Linda asked her friends if they knew any people who wanted to adopt a baby. One friend, named Esther Sue, knew a couple who did. Jerry and Linda met the adoptive parents and approved. Rose wanted to meet them, and she thinks the adoptive parents wanted to meet her, but Jerry would never allow it. He told her, "You don't need to meet them. It will be too much on you." Most likely, he was afraid Rose would reveal to them that he was the father, since they would be the adoptive parents. He would never arrange a meeting.

Jerry lied to Rose and told her the adoptive parents would be moving and couldn't meet with her. She was led to believe they were moving far away and would take the baby with them. They didn't move far away, and still lived close to that community until recently.

Jerry picked out the lawyer—one located in Elberton, which was farther away than either Hartwell or Royston. He thought this would be best "to keep from more embarrassment" for Rose, he said. Rose believes it was to keep anybody from finding out that he was the father. Rose didn't name the father in the adoptive papers. The lawyer kept asking if she was sure that she didn't want to include the father's name in the papers.

"The father has rights to this baby. The father has a right to know it's his, and that it's here," he said.

"The father knows it's his and it's here," Rose said. "I do not want to include the father in the process whatsoever." She did not want Jerry "ever, _ever_, **ever**" to "get his paws on [the baby], or be able to see him or anything. I want him to be far away from Jerry where Jerry cannot touch him at all," Rose said. The lie Jerry told her about the adoptive couple moving made Rose feel that the baby would be that much safer.

The adoptive couple paid for her hospital and doctor's bills, as well as the adoption fees. Everything was taken care of months before the birth. The lawyer kept telling Rose that she had not signed anything, and couldn't sign anything till after the birth, and that at any time, if she changed her mind, that he left a clause in the papers stating she could have her baby back within a year of the birth.

Rose had such a peace about giving the baby up that she couldn't change her mind. She knew this was what God wanted. Even while the child was still in her womb, she would sing to him, and talk to him, telling him that she loved him and always would, and that she would always pray for him. Just as Rose's grandmother prayed for her, Rose and her husband still pray for Rose's baby—for his salvation, that God will bless him, and that God will bring him a good, Christian woman to be his wife someday.

Rose would tell the baby in the womb that this (the adoption) was what she thought was best, and that God wanted her to do this. "I do truly love you," she would pray.

During the delivery, she felt lonelier than she ever had. She didn't know what to expect. She had not had any childbirth classes. Only the nurses and the doctor were in the delivery room with her, and they weren't there the whole time. She felt all alone and really depressed. "That was the most lonely time in my life," she recalls.

Her son was born in May, 1989, at Ty Cobb hospital in Royston. She isn't certain if he was born on the seventh or the ninth. She doesn't know how much he weighed, or how long he was. She only held him for a couple of minutes. She sang her song to him, one to which she would make up the words, melody, and tune as she went along. She then prayed over him and gave him a kiss. "God bless you, and be with you, and protect you for the rest of your life," she prayed.

"I still pray for him daily, even though he is not with me or with my husband or with my children. I know he's being taken care of, and I know that his mom and his dad do love him. They are his parents because they have raised him from a baby," she insists. She gave him his first name, the adoptive parents giving him the middle one, and theirs for the last. She felt he was a gift of God, and gave him a name with that meaning.

The adoptive parents took the baby home. Rose stayed in the hospital as long as she could—longer than she was supposed to stay. They finally told her she had to leave. She was so depressed. She didn't want to go back into Jerry and Linda's house, but knew that she had to return.

The day after her son was born, Ed came to visit Rose in the hospital. He gave her a single red Rose and a kiss on the cheek. "I'm thinking about you, and I'm here for you" he told her. "I'll always be your friend."

The lawyer knocked on the door and told who he was. Rose told Ed he had to leave the room.

"Are you sure you want to go through with this? Once you sign this paper, he will not be yours," the lawyer repeated.

Rose assured him she knew what was going on and that she knew he was just doing his job. Rose signed the papers, and the lawyer left. Ed returned, but she was so tired from having given birth to her son the day before that she couldn't talk long. She fell asleep, and she never saw him again. She has wondered ever since what happened to him, where he is, and why he never came back.

Jerry and Linda came in to visit Rose, though she would rather they had not. Stephanie came home from college to visit her in the hospital.

Rose would find out later that the adoptive couple had sent her a dozen roses and a white teddy bear with the baby's hospital picture in it, his name on the picture. They also sent her a note saying that they were glad that she gave birth to him instead of aborting him. They promised to take care of him. They told her their names and that they had adopted another son earlier, so he wouldn't be an only child—he would have a brother.

They thanked Rose for choosing them to raise him as a real son. Jerry did not let Rose have the flowers or the bear. Linda told Rose about it weeks later. Rose never saw them, though. Linda had kept the letter and the picture, and gave them to Rose when Rose finally left the D___s forever.

CHAPTER SEVEN

Rose returned to Jerry and Linda's house. She was very depressed. She absolutely did not want to be there. "Lord, please! I don't want to do anything else with him. I just want out."

Jerry told her he would wait until she was healed up before he would touch her again. She knew he would, because he had always left her alone when he said he would.

Rose never allowed him to do anything to her again. When he said he wanted to start having sex with her again, she finally told Linda that he was coming onto her, though she didn't say they had been having sex for six years, or that the boy was Jerry's. Linda tried to get him to stop, saying that Rose already had one baby; she didn't need another one.

Before Rose's six week check-up, Jerry confronted Linda. "Linda, I want you to know that I want to have Rose as my mistress," he said, after calling Rose and Linda into his bedroom and shutting the door. "I want to have sex with her. I love Rose."

"I thought you thought of her as a daughter," Linda protested.

"I do think of her as a daughter."

"Then, how can you have sex with her if you think of her as a daughter?"

"She meets my needs. I need someone to meet my needs because you don't. I want Rose, not you. You can never satisfy me sexually."

"Well, I can go have that operation to tighten up those muscles. I can lose weight and try to get back to the way I looked when we first got married." Rose still said nothing. "You don't have to use her like that," Linda insisted.

"Yes, I do. Even if you did do that, you would never satisfy me. I want Rose. I want what I want. I love you. You've been a good wife and a good mother to my children. I will always love you and I always want to be married to you. I always want us to live together and grow old together, and be husband and wife. You're a good wife and mother. You just don't satisfy me sexually and I need to be satisfied sexually. Rose does that and that's what I want."

"But, don't you love her as your daughter?"

"Yes, I do, but this is what I need."

"You wouldn't have sex with Stephanie would you?"

"No," he said, not mentioning that he had started with Stephanie before Rose came to live with them.

"And she's you're daughter. If you love Rose like a daughter, you shouldn't want to have sex with her. You wouldn't have sex with your boys and you love them."

"This is different. This is my outlet. Do you want me to go find someone outside the house and it get around that I'm having an affair on you? We'll get talked about around town. If I get caught, [the other foster child] will get taken away from us and he don't have anywhere to go. I think this is best for all of us. Rose is over eighteen now and she can make her own decisions. Let her decide what she wants to do."

Both of them turned to Rose and asked, "What do you want to do?"

Rose began crying. "I don't want to have sex with you! I don't want any part of it! I don't want to be your mistress!"

"Well, I'll treat you like a real foster child, then, like you should be treated and like other foster children are treated."

He started acting really cold to Rose. He wouldn't talk to her except to order her to go clean the bathroom, and he wouldn't let her out. She would have to stay in there until he left the house. He would give her evil looks, but said nothing else to her.

"I'm proud of you for sticking to your guns," Linda told Rose. "Don't let down."

Rose went to work for a couple of days after the six weeks period was over. Jerry was still being hard on the children, and cold toward Rose.

Finally, he called Rose to his bedroom. She went, knowing he wouldn't do anything to her. All the outside doors were open and Linda was home. It was still daylight. She knew he wouldn't risk it under these circumstances. He left the door open, too.

"I really need you. I want to have sex with you. I've been feeling a lot of pressure lately and I need to relieve this pressure," he said. "I love you. Think about [the other foster child]; where would he go? If you leave and [the child care organization] found out about this, they would take him away. What would happen to him? He'd be put in a group home and that would destroy him and his life.

"Where would you go? Your aunt doesn't want you. Your mom can't take care of you. Your brother and sister can't afford to take care of themselves, much less you. There is no safe place for you to go." Rose kept repeating that she didn't want to have sex with him.

Later that evening, he called Linda and Rose back into his bedroom. He told Linda that Rose had said yes to being his mistress, though she had insisted that she would never have sex with him again. He was planning to force her to have sex with him and be his mistress in spite of her resistance.

"Rose has agreed to be my mistress," he lied. "That's the way it's going to be, and you'll just have to accept it."

"You don't need to have sex with her. She's already had one baby. She doesn't need another one. You don't need to have sex with her, especially without any kind of protection."

"Well, I'll go get her some."

"She's already had one child. She doesn't need to be put through that again. Why would you want to choose her anyway?"

"I know she can satisfy me. We've already been having sex. [Rose's baby] is mine."

Linda began crying. "Rose doesn't need to have sex with you again. You don't need to be doing that. I won't stand by and let it continue to go on."

"You have no choice, and neither does Rose. Whether she wants to or not, I'm going to make her have sex with me. She will be my mistress."

They all decided at this point to go to bed because they all had to go to work the next day. The boys had been in bed already.

Rose and Linda went to work together the next day. They decided to leave Jerry that day. They left work and picked up the three boys. They packed what they could. It was at this time Linda finally gave Rose the picture and note from the adoptive parents and told her about the flowers and the bear, which Rose never saw.

Linda called Mike and Denise at the main campus. She was crying. She told them briefly what had happened and that she wanted to leave before Jerry got back from work.

Mike and Denise told her it would be better not to come in her own car. She took them to the relief shelter close by and hid her car behind it. Mike and Denise drove from the main campus and carried all five of them to the main campus that night.

Linda called Stephanie at her apartment at college and told her not to come home for any reason whatsoever. Stephanie still said nothing to her mom about what she and Jerry had done. Linda didn't tell Stephanie where they were going so Jerry could not find out from her. She told her that if Jerry called her, just tell him they had an emergency and had to leave.

Shane, the eldest son of Mike and Denise, talked with Rose alone. "I'm so sorry this happened. I have always felt like you were my sister. I'm so sorry." He held Rose and they both cried.

Mike and Denise begged Linda not to call Jerry. She was crying and kept saying, "Well, he'll be lonely. He'll be by himself."

"Give him a few days to think about what he has done," Mike and Denise told her.

"If you go back, we're not going back," said Greg and Brian. They hated their dad for what he had done. Brian, especially, didn't want to go back, for what Jerry did to Rose and for the way Jerry had been treating him.

They all stayed at the main campus a few more days. "You know you're going to have to leave [the other foster child] here, don't you?" Mike and Denise asked Linda.

"I know," she said. The other foster child was upset by having to stay at the main campus, but Rose thinks he took it pretty well.

Mike and Denise told Linda not to go back because Jerry didn't deserve her. They told her they would call and see how he was doing.

"Do you know where my wife and kids are?" Jerry asked them. "If you do, tell them I love them and I miss them. If they are up there with you, tell Linda to call me."

Mike and Denise kept telling her she didn't need to go back to Jerry. They told her she had plenty of grounds for divorce and that God would approve of it, even showing her the Scriptures where Jesus okayed divorce in cases such as adultery and sexual immorality.

"God will punish him for this. He will get Jerry for this," they assured her, correctly.

"But I still love Jerry! He's my husband. He's been my husband for [however many years it had been]. I trust him and I love him. I don't know what to do," she said in tears. She sneaked off and called Jerry, who convinced her to come back, as many gullible women do who are in abusive situations. Despite what they think, having a husband or boyfriend who is a horrible monster and is abusive is not better than going on without him. How often does the news cover a story where an abusive husband or boyfriend kills his or his girlfriend's child, molests them, or abuses her? Too often.

Brian cried and begged Mike and Denise to keep him.

"We don't have the authority. I'm sorry," they told him. "We can't interfere because Jerry and Linda would have to give up rights to you, and they won't."

After staying a total of four or five days, they all hugged Rose good-bye, telling her they were sorry this had happened to her. They returned to Jerry. The boys swapped addresses with the other foster child so that they could write each other. Rose didn't, to remain untraceable.

By this time, the main campus did finally have apartments for teenagers. They gave her the choice of staying there, and working somewhere close until she could go on her own, since she was twenty, or she could go stay with the Tolberts. They had called the Tolberts, who said they would be glad for Rose to stay there.

Rose said she would prefer to live with the Tolberts. She liked them. They had always been nice to her, and she knew she liked going to Pastor Glen's church.

"Maybe I can see Bill J. again," she thought to herself, "and have a normal life finally." She thought about going to college.

Mike and Denise asked Rose if she wanted to take legal action. She could have sued Jerry for what he had done to her. Stephanie begged Rose, "Please don't send my daddy to prison." She was still more concerned with her dad's welfare than that her "friend" had been tortured six years by him.

Rose could have also sued the childcare organization and DFACS for not doing their jobs. "No," she said, "the Lord says, 'Vengeance is mine, I will repay.' He can do more to them than I ever could. I'll leave it in His hands." She didn't think she could take being in the same room with him again, anyway, so she had rather not take any legal action. Still, she was assured that Jerry could never keep foster children again.

Some people might wonder why Rose was still faithful to God after all she had been through. "He never did anything to get her out of there in six years," they might say. That isn't true. It is like a story the authors have heard:

> There was an old man sitting on his front porch, reading his Bible. It was raining heavily and was beginning to flood. His neighbors ran by, shouting, "You'd better get to higher ground while you have the chance. It's still raining and it's supposed to keep on going. Come on with us."
>
> "No, God will take care of me," he replied, so they left him there.
>
> A little while later, the waters were up to his porch. A man in a boat came by and shouted, "You'd better come with me to higher ground where it's safe. It's still raining, and will keep on raining."
>
> "No, God will take care of me," he replied, so the man left him there.
>
> A little while later, the waters were up to his roof. A patrol boat came by and saw him sitting on his roof. They shouted, "You'd better come with us to higher ground where it's safe."
>
> "No, God will take care of me," he replied, so they left him there.
>
> A very little while later, he was standing on his chimney, the water up to his chest. A helicopter came flying over and lowered a rope ladder. The rescuer in back shouted down, "You'd better come with us to higher ground where it's safe."
>
> "No, God will take care of me," he replied, so they left him there.
>
> A very, very little while later, the man stood before God in heaven. "You let me down!" he yelled at God. "I trusted you. I told everyone you would take care of me and you didn't!"
>
> "You dummy," replied God, "I sent your neighbors, two boats, and a helicopter. What more did you want?"

Rose could have told any of her teachers in those six years. She could have told her best friend Becky. She could have talked to her pastor, or gotten back in touch with Mylon LeFevre after Jerry started back on her. She could have revealed what was happening to her to the Tolberts, or Mike and Denise. She could have told her caseworker. She could have told Bill J., or written to him and asked his help. She could have said something to the other Bill, or even Ed, who assured her that he was her friend.

God sent her a bunch of people from whom she could have gotten help. Rose didn't have the courage to do it. If anyone is going through any kind of abusive situation, God will bring people in front of you that you can tell and get help. Please tell someone. If they do like Linda and Stephanie did and don't get you help right away, tell someone else. Get help. As God told many people in the Bible, "Do not be afraid. Take courage. I will be with you." He loves you. He wants you out of those situations. Get out, please!

"But where was He when those things were being done to me?" someone might ask. That person has every right to ask God such a question. God won't get angry. He understands.

When the person goes through such situations, God is right there, shedding tears. His love for that person, for you, is greater than you can ever imagine.

He allows some people to go through such horrible times so that He can show them that, no matter what, He still cares for them. A popular poem puts it this way:

> One night a man had a dream. He dreamed he was walking along the beach with the Lord. Across the sky flashed scenes from his life. For each scene, he noticed two sets of footprints in the sand; one belonged to him, and the other to the Lord. When the last scene of his life flashed before him, he looked back at the footprints in the sand. He noticed that many times along the path of his life there was only one set of footprints. He also noticed that it happened at the very lowest and saddest times in his life. This really bothered him and he questioned the Lord about it.
>
> "Lord, you said that once I decided to follow you, you'd walk with me all the way. But I have noticed that during the most troublesome times in my life, there is only one set of footprints. I don't understand why when I needed you most you would leave me."
>
> The Lord replied, "My precious, precious child, I love you and I would never leave you. During your times of trial and suffering, when you see only one set of footprints, it was then that I carried you."
>
> —Author Unknown

Also, He allows a few to go through things so that they can tell others about it so that the person who did those things can never do them to anyone again.

He allowed Rose to go through her trial so that Jerry could not have any other foster children and do the same to them. Also, the child care organization and DFACS have gotten more strict and follow the rules more since Rose went through her six years of hell, so that hopefully, no other children have to suffer what she suffered.

He allowed Rose to suffer what she suffered because He knew her heart—that she loved Him—and He knew that one day, when she had healed spiritually, physically, and emotionally, she would have the courage to tell her story and help other girls and boys, men and women, who have endured similar circumstances. He knew that she would tell her story and could help many more know that their lives are not ruined, that God loves them, and that they can live normal lives in happiness.

Rose's story, then, is only half over. How did she get from a woman with no self-esteem, who lived in terror of her tormentor, broken from her abuse, to a woman of courage and love without fear? What did she go through after she left the D___s that aided this transformation? Read on...

Rosalee & T. Christopher Jarrell

CHAPTER EIGHT

Rose decided not to sue Jerry. "I just didn't have enough self-esteem, enough courage, enough strength, or anything to do it. God knew this, so I just left it alone," she admits.

The childcare organization decided they would pay for her to have oral surgery to correct her "buck teeth." They said they also had a grant from the contributions of people that was specifically for education, so they would pay for her to go to college, if she wanted.

Rose doesn't know if they offered to do these things because they were really sorry for what had happened to her, or because they were afraid she would sue them, and so did it as a peace offering to appease her and keep her quiet. She assumed the best. She knows they help a lot of children, and bears no ill feelings against the organization or DFACS because of her situation.

Very few children at the time, however, knew about this grant, so the money often went unused. Many foster children don't have the self-esteem to believe they can go to college, and don't see how they can pay for it. This organization did have the funds to send children who had stayed with them to college. Rose hopes they tell more children about it now.

The day after Linda, Greg, and Brian returned to Jerry, Rose went to live with the Tolberts in Douglasville. Rose didn't want the D___s to know where she was, and so decided to wait until Linda and the two boys left before she did. She could have gone immediately to live with the Tolberts, but she wanted to know what Linda would do first.

When Rose arrived at the Tolberts, she told them everything that had happened—all six years of it. She only told Grandmother and Paw-paw. She doesn't know if they told anyone else. Nobody ever acted like they had.

"We wish we had known," they told her. "We're sorry it happened. You could have come to live with us anytime. We wish we had stressed that point to you. We're sorry we didn't."

Rose enjoyed life with them. They went to church at Soul's Arbor. Pastor Glen called her "Sissy" (meaning "sister") because she was staying with his mom.

Rose began looking for a school to attend. Her caseworker said, "Well, I know a little school. It is in the country. It doesn't have a lot of students. It's safe. You'll be safe there. Let me take you down there for a look."

The school was Gordon College in Barnesville. It is a two-year school in a small town. Rose liked the looks of it. The child-care organization pushed Rose to go to school there, mainly to help hide her from Jerry.

"You're in time to go this fall if you can go ahead and get your SAT scores in," the caseworker said. They rushed to get Rose's test. Rose was accepted for admittance that fall—the fall of 1989. Her son had been born in May. She had left the D___s in mid June, and had gone to live with the Tolberts at the end of June or the beginning of July. Now she was making plans to attend college that September. Being accepted to college helped Rose believe she was smart enough to go to college despite six years of Jerry saying she wasn't.

Paul's granddaughter, Lagina, was staying with them already, and Rose shared a room with her. She was still in high school. They got along together fairly well. The Tolberts had a pool behind the house, so they went swimming often.

Grandmother Tolbert took Rose shopping to prepare for school that fall. The child-care organization sent her an allowance so she could buy some things. They bought sheets, a pillow, underwear, and some nice clothes. Rose loved this! She hadn't been able to go shopping for her own clothes while living with the D___s.

The child-care organization had paid the D___s monthly for being foster parents and to take care of Rose's medical bills and her personal needs. For her birthdays and holidays, the organization would send money to buy presents for Rose, and sent a few presents, too. Rose only got these presents. Jerry kept the money every time for himself during those six years. The child-care organization threatened to sue Jerry after Rose left because he had misappropriated those funds. Rose doesn't know if they carried through with their threats, though.

The Tolberts, by contrast, would not only spend the money sent to them for Rose on Rose, but they spent above and beyond that out of their own pockets.

Rose went to Soul's Arbor as often as she could. She loved attending there. "It was good for me spiritually, and it was good for me healing-wise, also—like a healing process," she said.

Lagina went back to high school in August. Every morning, the girls (including Grandmother) got up and did their chores before daylight. If Grandmother planned to go shopping that day, they went. Otherwise, they would clean up the house and then relax for the rest of the day, sometimes going swimming.

When September came, Grandmother, Paw-paw, Rose, and her caseworker all drove to Gordon. The caseworker had the check for Rose's tuition, room and board, books, and fees. She and Rose both had to sign it. There was money left over, which Rose left in her account at the school in case she needed paper or pencils, and for her other needs.

Grandmother especially wanted to meet Rose's roommate at the dorm. Since it was not a coed dorm, Paw-paw had to stay in the lobby. When they got to the room, which was on the first floor, facing away from the classroom buildings and toward the parking lot, they discovered that Rose's roommate, Liz, had already claimed her side and had completely set up her stuff. Her bed was already made, the clothes were in the closet, and the refrigerator was cooling.

"Boy, she's fast!" Rose thought to herself. "She must have gotten here early this morning." It was about 3 or 4 p.m. by the time Rose had gotten there.

The beds were twin sized and about three feet from the ceiling, not allowing much room to move around. Under each bed was a desk on one side, and a closet on the other, which helped support the bed. The ladder went up the side of the closet. The desk had a couple of shelves over it and a light. It was a deep desk with deep drawers. Pictures could be hung beside the desk on the back of the closet.

The two bed units were pushed together in one corner, one on one wall, and one on the adjacent wall. The window was beside Liz's bed, the sink and mirror across from it. Rose's bed was opposite the window, and a large air-conditioner/heater unit hung over her feet, giving her even less space. The door to the room was at the foot of Rose's bed, next to her closet. The room had old carpet and cinder block walls. The dormitory itself had several floors, with all its rooms about the same as Rose's.

"I always thought Liz was pretty," Rose admits, "though she was weird." Liz studied a lot and hard, which was good for Rose for her first year. Liz wasn't a party animal, attending every party as many others did. Many of the other students would drink at night and on weekends just to get drunk, and would be too hung over to attend class the next day. Liz did not do this, for which Rose was thankful.

"She was a character, though," Rose testifies. Liz wanted the two of them to take aerobics together, but Rose already had her schedule. They ate meals together, but this was Liz's second year and Rose's first, so they didn't have classes together. Rose even went home with Liz some weekends, when Liz's mother would allow it. Rose was having a good first year at college, enjoying her newfound freedom. Chris, however, was just beginning his twelfth-grade year, and things had been terrible for him lately.

He had been praying for Rose since seventh grade at twelve years old. Rose had been sixteen and in ninth grade at the same time—the 84-85 school year. His grandfather on his mother's side had died in 1984 of emphysema from years of smoking.

A short time into his eighth grade year, still in 1985, Chris' house burned. The house was a total loss, though a few of their belongings were recovered. He still has his seventh grade yearbook, which is smoke-damaged and smells like smoke to this day.

The family had gone to Macon from Monticello to eat dinner at Pizza Hut. On the way home, Chris rode with his dad in his "boom truck," the truck he used at work for General Tire. It had a large, powerful crane on the back of it so that he could change the huge tires from loaders and earthmovers. Some of the tires were large enough for his dad to stand inside and reach up, still unable to touch the top of the tire.

Chris and his dad passed a black church which had a car stuck in the ditch. Its back tire had gone in the ditch and the people were struggling in vain to get it out. As he always did, Chris' dad stopped to help.

Chris remembered that once before, a car had flipped over in a large ditch down the road from his house. A crowd surrounded it. A little boy was still trapped inside, his arm outside of the car, pinned between the roof of the car and the ground. Police, an ambulance, and other rescuers had tried in vain to free the boy. They were now planning to hook a tow truck to it and drag it sideways to free the boy. This would completely crush his arm and sever it, causing him to lose it permanently. Chris' dad, Tom, talked them into waiting until he ran home, about a block away, and got his truck to see what he could do.

He hooked chains to the axles of the car and looped them over the hook on the "boom," or crane. Then he picked the car straight up, allowing rescue workers to get the boy out. The boy's arm had only minor damage, and he only needed to wear a cast for a while.

Afterwards, Tom merely said, "Where do you want the car?" He could place it anywhere the boom could reach. He didn't accept anything for helping.

"The truck did all the work," he said.

Now, he had stopped to help at the church. He discovered they had been having a dinner, when the passenger in the car had gotten a bone lodged in his throat. They were trying to rush him to the hospital. Who knows why they didn't wait for an ambulance! He picked up the back of the car and pushed it forward so that it rested securely on the ground. Again, he took no reward.

When they arrived home, their house was gone except for the floor and outside walls. Fire trucks surrounded it. One of Chris' friends, Jeremy, had been across the street, visiting a girlfriend. He had paused during a smooching session with her on the front porch long enough to see smoke coming from Chris' house. He called the fire department, but it was too late. The house was almost a century old, so the wood was almost pure kindling, like the wood used to start fires because it burns quickly and easily.

Chris left with relatives to stay in Douglasville that night. That is where all the family on his mom's side was from, and where his aunts, uncles, and grandmother lived, as well as a bunch of cousins. Chris was more worried about his dogs, purebred beagles, than anything else. They were fine.

In the next few years, Chris and his family would move to different rental homes many times. For the rest of his eighth grade year, from January till June, he would live with his grandmother, known as Granny, and attend school in Douglasville at Stewart Middle School. He hated that school. He was constantly bullied there because of his intelligence and good grades.

He had not always done well in school. He had a problem of bedwetting and wetting on his clothes all the way to the middle of first grade. Once, in kindergarten, the teacher's aid, a mean lady that terrified Chris, told the boys to go brush their teeth in the bathroom after lunch, but that they had better not play or use the bathroom. Chris really had to go, and all that running water didn't help! He stood there during and after brushing his teeth, holding himself and dancing around trying not to potty on himself. The other boys told him to go to the bathroom anyway, but he was too scared. He eventually lost it, completely soaking his pants. He began crying.

When he finally came out of the bathroom, still crying, the teacher, a nice older black woman named Ms. Goolsby, who was nearing retirement, gave Chris a hug anyway and told him it would be okay. He had to go home in wet, smelly clothes, though, and all the kids made fun of him.

Then, in first grade, while riding the bus home, it hit him—he had to go, but his house was miles away. They got close to his house, but it was in a winding subdivision and he didn't know the way (they wouldn't have let him off early anyway). He lost it half a mile from his house, soaking his pants and his seat. The other kids laughed at him.

Finally, his mother took him to a doctor about it. The doctor said he'd cut the opening of the penis to enlarge it and see if that helped. Chris dropped his pants. The doctor put one side of the scissors in and clamped down, then dropped the scissors (which were still attached to Chris), onto the examining table. He was sitting there with a big, cold, heavy pair of scissors hanging from his "wee-wee." It wasn't a pleasant experience. This still didn't stop the problem.

Chris was entered into the hospital. They ran tests, took X-rays, and then put him to sleep with some peppermint-flavored gas. He awoke with a tube coming out of his "wee-wee" connected to a plastic bag. His self-esteem was already shot, and even though the nurses flirted with him and said he was cute, it didn't help his six-year-old self-image, especially since they kept pulling up his gown to check on his front while his back was exposed for everyone else to see.

When the time came to remove the tube and bag, the nurses assured him it would be okay. They laid him in a dimly lit room. A stocky nurse, who talked very soothingly, pulled his gown up and yanked a ten-foot tube out of his two-inch penis (of course, things look larger than they really are to a child—the tube, I mean). Again, this wasn't a pleasant experience. Chris screamed and cried, but she hugged him, and he soon stopped. He bled and burned and hurt for days after that, but he didn't wet the bed, or himself, again.

His family always seemed to be moving while he was growing up. He had missed half of kindergarten and the end of first grade because of two separate moves. By second grade, he was far behind everyone else. For example, it took him almost the whole year of second grade to figure out "greater than" and "less than." He couldn't figure out what "alligator" his teacher kept mentioning was, and what did she mean by it kept swallowing the larger numbers?

He almost failed second grade. He felt completely stupid. They tested him for intelligence, as they did for the rest of the class. A few students were pulled aside for an accelerated reading program during class everyday. Chris was one of them. They had a list of books to read, while the other students had only one or two to read. The teacher would ask those in the accelerated reading program how far they were in their current book, and ask them questions about their reading. Chris had no desire to read. "What's the use? I'm too stupid anyway," he thought.

While the other students were quickly finishing books and getting little ribbons and smiley faces on their papers, Chris still hadn't completed the first chapter of the first book. He was making "D" minuses consistently in his other subjects, too. Most of the way through the year, he still hadn't read the first book on the list. Dick and Jane were too boring, and he thought he was too stupid.

He was getting very ashamed of himself for not reading. The other four or five students in the program were almost finished with their lists, and still, he was on the first book. He finally decided he would try, but still felt too stupid. He plodded along slowly through that book. He just didn't feel capable of doing well. He was learning phonics, this being the last year it would be taught to him, so he knew how to sound out words and discover their meanings even if he had never seen them before, but that didn't make him confident.

He finally figured out a method of doing math that he could use. The teacher wouldn't let him count on his fingers and toes, so he had to do something. One workbook showed objects grouped together and various things were done with those groups—addition, subtraction, multiplication, and division. Chris learned to envision those same objects in groups in his mind and move them around to get the answers.

After doing this for a while, he got to where he didn't have to see objects in his mind, but could still see numbers in his head in groups and could manipulate them to get the answers.

When the class moved to using a flat line with the mathematical sign and numbers for math, Chris quickly adapted his method to this. He would envision the flat line in his mind with the sign and numbers in the appropriate places and could perform the correct calculations totally in his mind. When he was taught long division in third grade, he adapted this in his mind, too.

By his senior year, Chris could multiply and divide two numbers, each one three wide, and get the correct answer faster in his mind than his teacher or classmates could while using a calculator. (By his senior year of college, however, he could barely multiply double digits in his head.) His method of doing math in his head would prove very useful in years to come. He would teach it to Rose, which helped her self-image and enabled her to do well in future employment.

Even though he could do all of this, Chris still made D minuses and hadn't finished his first book. He just had no self-esteem.

Years later, while attending a "Young Marrieds" Sunday School class, two of Chris' teachers repeatedly said they did not like the term self-esteem. The Bible uses the term, though, in a positive way, so Chris doesn't see the problem that they had with it. The Bible tells us not to esteem ourselves more highly than we ought. This does not mean that self-esteem is wrong, but thinking too much of ourselves is wrong. It is also harmful to esteem ourselves lower than we ought. This was what was happening to Chris and Rose.

The best course, then, is for everyone to esteem himself or herself correctly—we are all created by God in His image, so we are of great value, so much so that He died for us. At the same time, we are all sinners who cannot get to heaven on our own—we are neither better nor worse than anyone else. We are all in the same boat—lost and in need of a Savior, the Lord Jesus Christ.

In addition to Chris having low self-esteem from everything else, the girls kept calling him names. He began hating all girls, except for the high school girls. When they talked to him, he'd just blush and lower his head.

Then, about a month before second grade ended, something happened that would change Chris forever. He got a "D" plus! He was so excited that he hugged his teacher! He showed several students, "Look, a 'D' plus, not a 'D' minus!" He knew he could do this school stuff then. He quickly finished the first book on the list and about two others, but then the year ended. He was at the bottom of his class.

By the end of third grade, he had the highest average. For fourth grade, he tied with "that girl!"—the one whom he would consider his nemesis, his archrival—Daphne. He did well for fifth, sixth, and seventh grades, but wasn't told the rankings. He was getting pretty confident. Then came eighth grade.

Those six months at Stewart in Douglasville was horrible. Several boys decided they didn't like Chris because he was a "nerd." They would knock his books onto the floor, trip him, throw one of his books over his head to each other, and push him around. He begged his mom to move back to Monticello, where his friends were. He had never been treated like this there. She wouldn't do it, though, saying everything would be all right.

Then one day, as Chris was walking down the hall to class, the lead boy—a blond, longhaired punk with an earring—walked up to Chris from a side hall and punched him in the eye. Chris had not said anything to him or done anything to him. Chris didn't even see the boy until he had been hit. Chris had tried to act friendly to the boy before, but it obviously hadn't worked. Chris couldn't fight, so he just stood there, shocked. The boy said something mean to him and walked off.

When he got home, Chris told his mom what had happened. "I won't go back there," he said. "If you make me, I won't go past this year, even if I have to run away. Take me back to Monticello, or I won't go back to school!"

She made him go back the next day, saying she would take care of it. He went back to school, but tucked a sharp pointed pen under his wristband on his right arm. Nobody could see it while he held his fingers straight, but if he made a fist, it poked out an inch past his fingers.

"If he tries to hurt me again, I'll hit him as hard as I can in his eye. I don't care if he goes blind, or I kill him—I'm tired of being treated like this," he told himself.

To Chris' surprise, all the boy and his companions did was give him evil looks. They said nothing to him and didn't come close to him. The assistant principle called over the intercom in one class for Chris to come to the office. Chris didn't remember doing anything wrong. "What do they want with me?" he wondered.

"Chris," the man said in his office, after closing the door, "your mother called and told me what happened yesterday and that if it happened again, she'd have the 'little hoodlum' arrested. I've already talked to the boy. If he or any of his companions or anyone else ever bothers you again, just let me know." They never did bother him again.

Chris recalled this incident years later when he read a bumper sticker that was in response to those saying, "My child is an honor roll student at Such and Such school." These stickers read, "My kid beat up your honor roll student." Chris wanted to have some printed up to read, "Yeah, but my honor roll student will be your brat's parole officer," but, as yet, he has not followed through with this.

With all the school violence that has occurred in the past few years, Chris is glad that those bullies were stopped before things got to the point where he actually did retaliate, though, at the time, he was ready to do so with even one more occurrence.

CHAPTER NINE

Even though Chris and his family moved back to Monticello that summer, the damage was done. Another incident at Stewart in Douglasville would affect him negatively before leaving.

For several years, Chris had problems with ingrown toenails on both feet so much so that he literally forgot how to walk. By eighth grade, he no longer had problems with ingrown toenails, but he was having trouble remembering how to walk without crutches and without limping from the operations on his feet. Some people at Stewart made fun of him for the way he walked, saying he walked like a "fag." Chris was very self-conscious about this, but was helpless to do anything.

Chris did well enough at Stewart to win a Presidential Academic Fitness award signed by Ronald Reagan (though it was probably only a stamp). At awards day, all the students were assembled in the gym. When his name was called, he got up and tried to control his walk so he wouldn't get laughed at by the whole school. As he walked up the rows to the platform, row after row began laughing at him.

"Look at the way he walks!" one student exclaimed.

"Fag!" another said, though Chris was definitely not a homosexual.

He heard the boy who had hit him yell, "Nerd!" and the punks who followed him all jeered and repeated the insult.

What had started as a proud moment quickly turned into a humiliating event. That summer, Chris would practice walking by himself. By the time ninth grade started, his walk had changed, but it still wasn't right. He now bounced six inches or more with every step. It would take Marine Corps boot camp to teach him to walk without such a pronounced bounce.

For the next four years, he would be compared to Disney's Goofy because of his walk. He could say, "Huh, garsh!" and sound close enough to get a laugh, so he could live with it. At least it was better than being called a fag because of his walk. Still, because of his experiences at Stewart, he determined never again to be an object of ridicule because of good grades. He stopped trying in school, and in French class, tried to do poorly.

Ninth grade started and his old unofficial girlfriend, the girl who had wanted to teach him what "sex" was, walked into the room. His heart jumped. He recognized her instantly. She, however, had no memory of who he was or even of that time. She said her parents had divorced and she had blocked all that out. She didn't even act like she liked Chris.

Instead, she started going with one of Chris' three best friends, Johnny (later, he would want to be called John, but Chris still calls him Johnny). This hurt

Chris, especially since he had hoped to marry her someday. All his hopes were dashed. He knew God had him praying for someone else, but still he had hoped.

He knew he could resist this girl's attempts to tempt him to have sex with her. Chris also knew his friend Johnny. He knew his friend wouldn't resist her, and if she didn't offer, he would push her to have sex with him. If she did offer, he would jump at the first chance to have sex with her.

Chris was staying a virgin for his future wife. He didn't want any girl who wouldn't do the same. What he knew would happen between this girl and Johnny disgusted him. He lost interest in her totally.

For the next few years, he would counsel girls on their relationships. He had spent most summers with his Granny. They would play Monopoly till four in the morning, sleep till noon, and then do it again. He had gone to the beauty parlor with her, listened to the gossip and the way women felt, get his cheeks pinched by those who were his Granny's age, and get free cokes from them because he was "such a good little boy." He had never had many close friendships, even with guys, and since God told him to pray for his future wife starting at age twelve, he had felt closer to girls.

Now, they would have relationships with guys who treated them like dirt. They knew they could trust Chris. His heart would beat wildly with each one. "She's so beautiful and so sweet. Lord, is she the one?" he'd pray silently. They never were.

They would come crying to him, telling him all that their jerk boyfriends had done. He would listen till they finished, sometimes giving them hugs, sometimes holding their hands, but always listening. When they asked him what they should do, if it were only a misunderstanding, he would try to reunite the couple—acting as arbitrator.

If they had really been mistreated, he would tell them to leave the jerks, they could do better. He would reassure them that they were beautiful, even though they insisted they weren't. He would tell them to look for someone who goes to church and treats them and everyone nicely and with respect. They usually didn't follow his advice. They would go back to the same dirtbags, get hurt again, then come back to Chris for more counseling and advice.

"I wish I could find someone just like you," they would say.

"Well here I am," he would think, but he said nothing. "Have you seen me with anyone? Does anyone call me her boyfriend? Come on! Get a clue!" he would think, but not utter a word.

It seemed to him what they meant was really, "I wish I could find someone just like you—just not you!"

When he did get up the nerve to ask some of them out, they would all say, "I think of you more as a brother than as a boyfriend." In other words, they wanted guys who would treat them like trash because their brothers didn't, but if anyone would love them, respect them, and treat them like queens, they didn't want those guys because their brothers acted similarly (or at least they pretended like their brothers did).

After several years of this treatment, Chris was frustrated. One girl told him the same "brother" line, and he replied, "No thanks, I have enough family," then slammed the phone down.

"Why don't girls like me?" he prayed. He never received an answer to that one.

Chris tried to act "cool" by cussing. Some students acted surprised, saying, "I didn't know you cussed."

His language got worse and worse until a very beautiful girl named Tonya, whom Chris liked and respected (and wanted to impress), looked at him and said, "Chris, that's not you!" He was so ashamed that he almost totally stopped cussing from then on, with only a few slip-ups since. He started saying things like "Dad-gummitt" and "Dad-burn-it" that he picked up from his Granny. When his five-year-old daughter was three and she got angry at something, she would look at it and say "gummitt!"

Even though Chris wasn't trying in school, he still made A's and B's in most classes. It still irritated him to make a B—"B's are boring," he said. He wouldn't try to improve, though. He was determined <u>not</u> to be made fun of because of his intelligence and grades.

He wouldn't admit that anyone was smarter than he, not even Daphne! If any other kids wanted help with their schoolwork or just weren't sure of themselves, Chris would encourage them and try to help them without giving them the answers. One of his favorite teachers, Mr. E., told him that just giving away answers was not teaching, and didn't help the person any. True teaching, he said, was helping them know how to solve the problem, and then letting them arrive at the answer themselves, though sometimes a little help is necessary to keep them on track.

The only foreign language class taught in Monticello was French. He didn't want to take any foreign language class, but was told he would have to take this one. In rebellion, he would purposefully mispronounce words with a definite Southern drawl. Most people say he still doesn't have an accent. His family says he has been "Yankyfied" by his teachers. Still, Chris can do a great redneck Southern when he chooses, and he so chose in French class.

For the first year, he made all low C's in that class. He continued until the next-to-the-last six weeks of his second year of French class. His parents, stating they knew he could do better if he tried, grounded him for the entire six weeks. His French grade went from 72 to 92, so they took him off of restriction for the last six weeks of the tenth grade. His grade dropped to a 70—and there were no D's in high school. Below a 70 was an F. 70 to 79 was a C. This was all the French Chris was required to take, so grounding him further was useless. His parents just left it alone.

Chris was still invited to awards night that year. He received a certificate of achievement as the one with the second highest average for a male. He was surprised by this, but later was told by the counselor that the only reason he got anything was because the reward was supposed to go to tenth graders and the top two girls and top two boys got the awards.

"You wouldn't have gotten it because there are so many girls ahead of you, but only the top two get awards, and you were second for boys, and we had to give the other two awards to boys," she said. This did not make him happy.

In his eleventh grade, he still wasn't willing to put forth much effort, except in one class—geometry. He kept making the same grade—85, a B—six weeks after six weeks. He was getting tired of it, so he decided to try, but he kept making B's whatever he did. He would try in class—get a B. He wouldn't try—get a B. He would do his homework—get a B. He wouldn't do his homework—get a B. He finished geometry for the year with "Surprise, surprise, surprise"—a B. He was not happy.

For the Junior/Senior prom that year, Chris wanted to take the most beautiful girl in the school, though she was three years younger than he was. He could talk to anybody well except her. When she walked by, she would smile her perfect smile and say, "Hi, Chris."

"Uh... um... duh... [sigh]... uh... hi," he would finally get out. The girls with whom this heavenly beauty walked would giggle and whisper about this older boy who was a bumbling idiot.

"How are you?" she asked.

"Duh... um... uh... okay." He wanted to converse with her and tell her how wonderful she was and would she like to go out sometime, but all he could do was stand there. His tongue got so thick he couldn't say anything. Chris adjusted his collar.

After about thirty seconds, she would finally say, "Well, I've got to go to class," and disappear in a door, the other girls still giggling.

"You dummy! She's just a girl. Why can't you talk to her?" he asked himself, barely aloud. He walked to his class, slapping himself on his forehead. He wondered if she were the one to be his future wife. If so, he didn't understand why his tongue refused to function properly in her presence.

The girl's mom and Chris' older sister talked Chris into calling her and asking her to the prom. They were good friends and the mother really liked Chris, supposedly because she knew that he would make a good husband for her daughter.

Chris called while his sister sat watching. The mother answered, happy that Chris called. She assured him that her daughter did not have a boyfriend and no one had asked her to the prom. She called her daughter to the phone to talk to Chris.

His heart about to explode, Chris asked her to be his date for the prom. Then, he felt like the clay target being shot into pieces in skeet shooting competitions when she said, "I'm sorry. I can't. I've had a boyfriend for a year now and I'm going to his prom. I'm sorry."

"That's okay," he lied. He hung up the phone and told his sister. She immediately called the girl's mom back and told her what had happened. They both apologized for talking him into asking the girl and for not knowing she had a boyfriend.

The next day, he asked a girl, whom he knew to be good friends with the girl he had asked, who this boyfriend was. She informed Chris that he went to the local private school and was a Senior there. He and the girl had been seeing each other on an "on-again-off-again" basis for over a year. They had been separated and had only gotten back together a few days before. That was why the girl's mom didn't know that she had a boyfriend.

Chris' sister, Melanie, took him for a weekend vacation the weekend of the prom to get his mind off this girl. It didn't work. They went to a private campground outside of Helen. He was miserable. They went to sit by the pool after dark. Chris lay down on the diving board on his stomach with his chin on his arms. He looked over the end of the board watching the light under the surface of the pool make weird shadowy shapes as the breeze made tiny waves on the water. His tears made small splashes in the pool as they hit, creating even more ripples. He hurt all over.

When Chris returned on Monday to school, the friend with whom he had talked before found him and informed him what had happened the night of the prom. The girl Chris had asked out had gone with her boyfriend and had had sex with him afterwards.

"Oh, I wish she had gone with you," she said, "because this never would have happened. He's such a jerk anyway. I don't know what she sees in him. I know you wouldn't have done anything with her."

Chris was crushed. The girl with whom he was infatuated had given herself willingly to a man out of wedlock. It made Chris nauseous. He would never have trouble talking to her again. He was no longer interested in her, nor would be ever again.

He had once thought of her as a beautiful flower in full bloom. Now, he could only think of her as a flower whose petals had all been picked, leaving only an ugly, dead, withered, and drooping stem.

"I don't want her," he told himself. "I'm saving myself for my future wife. I don't want a girl who can't do the same." It would take him almost a year to heal from the pain of having someone for whom he cared soil herself in such a way. She would not be his future wife.

Rosalee & T. Christopher Jarrell

CHAPTER TEN

To make matters worse, Chris' parents got a divorce at the end of his eleventh grade year. His mom had a nervous breakdown and left. They thought she was having an affair and left with a guy, but she really only went to her mom's.

His parents filed for a divorce, and within a month his dad was seeing another woman. They married before his divorce was final, but they would stay together for five years. She was an evil woman, making Cinderella's wicked stepmother seem like Mrs. Santa Claus. She had a daughter and two sons, one a year younger than Chris, the other was three.

They talked about ouija boards and magic. Their favorite holiday was Halloween. The girl and her mom wore black makeup and fingernail polish, and wore spider web earrings. They enjoyed evil and evil things. Since Chris was a Christian, they didn't get along very well.

The three year old was the worst brat Chris had ever seen. They refused to spank him for anything he did wrong, not even willing to slap his hand if he was trying to do something dangerous over and over. They tried to rationalize and talk with him to make him behave as if he were a college student and old enough to think rationally and be persuaded by argumentation. Consequently, he was out of control.

He still threw food, though he should have stopped over a year before. He would get into other people's rooms, even when they had locked their doors, and break their belongings.

He emptied a brand new bottle of Brut cologne, which belonged to Bill, Chris' little brother, onto Bill's books, while they were still in the bookshelf. He would flush things down the toilet and empty whole bottles of anything he could find, even if he had to climb to get them.

Cody, the three-year-old, dumped a whole jar of fish food into Chris' fish tank, killing every one of the fish. Chris couldn't even find all the bodies of his fish and had no idea what the little heathen did with those fish.

Elaine, the evil stepmother, wouldn't lift a finger or her voice to try to stop her demon child, but she happily abused Chris' little brother, Bill, and his little sister, Lynne. They told Chris what she was doing, but he didn't want to believe it at first. He decided to sneak around and investigate. He would go up the stairs to his room and shut the door, pretending to have gone in. He would creep part way down the stairs so that he couldn't be seen but could hear.

Elaine would hit Bill and Lynne and yell at them, which she would never do to her own children. She would grab Lynne's shoulders and shake her violently, yelling all the while. She did all this when Tom, Chris' dad wasn't around. Chris confronted his dad with what was happening, but instead of believing his own son, he accused Chris of trying to break up his new marriage. He told Chris he needed to start looking for another place to live.

Chris and Elaine were arguing regularly now, but since he was almost six-foot-tall and sixteen-years-old, she didn't dare try to push him around or hit him. He called her a witch often and a word that rhymes with it just as often, and both fit. Tom would tell his son not to call Elaine names, to which Chris would reply, "If the name fits, be called by it." Tom was trying harder to find somewhere for Chris to live now.

Chris often rode his bicycle down the road to the house of one of his English teachers, Mrs. A.. She had become a close and dear friend to him. He would go to her house and cry, talk about the situation in which he and his younger siblings were trapped, and seek advice.

Upon returning one night, he discovered that Tom and Elaine had gone and taken Cody. Michael, the other son, had taken his Trans Am out for the night. Bill and Lynne had been left with Kelly, the Satanic daughter. She had locked the doors and would not let Chris in. She stood there calling him names, sticking her tongue out at him, and "flipping him birds." He had not done anything to her to provoke her actions.

After thirty minutes of standing in front of his own front door, Chris had finally had enough. With one kick, the door flew open, but the lock was no longer functional. It hung loosely from its screw. Chris didn't touch Kelly, who stood there staring at Chris with an evil expression. He just walked past her and went upstairs, Bill and Lynne following. They felt safer with him than with Satan's daughter.

When Tom and Elaine returned, Tom stormed upstairs and began yelling at Chris as if he had started the incident. Of course, Chris yelled back that "Witch Number II" was at fault and shouldn't have locked him out.

Tom went back downstairs to try and fix the door. Chris heard Elaine telling Tom that Kelly shouldn't be left alone with Chris because he might "try something." Chris understood they were going to try to set him up and make it seem like he had raped Kelly, which he would never do. When he told Mrs. A. what was said, she agreed with Chris' understanding, and urged him not to be alone with her. "Always have a witness," she said.

When he called his mom, with whom he had finally gotten back in touch and found out what had happened to her, she urged him to keep Bill and Lynne with him at all times that he was home. He did this until Tom finally kicked him out.

Chris got invited to awards night his eleventh grade year. He expected to receive something, but when it ended, he hadn't gotten anything. "Why was I even invited?" he thought to himself. "I can't believe I didn't get anything. This will not happen again!" This, coupled with his parent's recent separation and having been told the year before that his average was second for a boy—but still behind a long list of girls—was all Chris could stand.

He spent most of the days that summer with a friend who was a year younger than he, Chris S., the son of another of his English teachers, Ms. S.. Her husband had committed adultery and left, and they, too, were divorced or in the process. The younger Chris, who had hated his mother for years, immediately took his dad's side, though it was his dad who had abandoned him and his mother for a younger woman. The elder Chris thought the man was a jerk and scum for doing this and couldn't understand why the younger Chris would take his side. Sure his mom tended to nag and be strict, but he usually brought it on himself by being hyper and not helping out around the house.

Still, the two Chrises got along because of their intelligence. They enjoyed playing computer games at school, the kinds where clues are given to solve mysteries. If one Chris would miss something, the other would catch it, and vice versa. They enjoyed figuring things out together. They also shared an interest in books about knights and chivalry.

Though the elder Chris was 265 pounds, slow, and out of shape, and the younger one was half his size, shorter, more hyper, faster, and in shape, they began sword-fighting daily during the summer. They took mulberry branches (mulberry held up better than anything else they tried) about two inches in diameter and four feet in length and would try as hard as possible to hit the other person. Headshots were outlawed, as were those in a sensitive area on males. Anywhere else was fair game.

They wore no gloves, no helmets, no pads (and no sense). They would fight as hard as possible for 2-3 hours a day, everyday, stopping only when one or the other got hit well enough to require a pause. The elder Chris lost 75 pounds during the summer and an additional 15 pounds the first two weeks of school. After that, he just toned up.

Before school started back, Chris went to talk to the guidance counselors. "What would it take for me to be Valedictorian?" he asked.

"That's impossible. Daphne has it sewn up. She's way ahead of everyone else because she's been consistent for four years. You haven't. There's no way to even catch up, much less pass her."

"Well, what would it take to be Salutatorian?"

"There's no way you can do that, either."

"What would it take?"

"You'd have to make 95 and above in every subject all year long."

"All right, then," he replied as he turned and left. That year, despite his problems at home, he made a few 95's and even fewer 96's. The majority of his classes were 97 and above. He even had one hundred averages for the year in both English and accounting.

When classes began, everyone who knew him the year before commented on his new size and looks. He enjoyed the attention, not having had it before. Things were going along well at school. Chris was elected to Student Council; President of the Science Club, in which he had participated for years; finally got accepted into Beta Club; and became co-editor of the Literary Magazine. Things were not going so well at home.

"Have you found anywhere to live yet?" Tom asked.

"No."

"Well, I know where you can stay. Start packing and I'll take you there in a few days."

Tom took Chris to stay with Charlie and Shirley E., members of their church, Bethel Baptist Church. They told Chris what the rules were, most of which he would never do, anyway, and made it sound as if he were a juvenile delinquent. Chris felt uncomfortable and unwanted there, even though they were nice to him. He got similar treatment from other adults around town. He realized that Tom had told several people in town that Chris was a problem child and, as always happens in a small town, the word got spread. It was now December of his Senior year, and Chris was miserable.

Chris stayed with the E.'s over the holidays. They were getting nicer to him, maybe realizing Chris wasn't the monster his dad had led people to believe. Still, they reminded Chris he could only stay a few weeks. Chris' mom urged him to move to Douglasville with her and finish school there. Chris absolutely wouldn't have it. He knew that he couldn't move anywhere in the last six months of his Senior year and expect to be Salutatorian or receive any kind of scholarship. Without scholarships, he could never afford college. He had to stay in Monticello.

Lynne and Bill would remain with Tom and Elaine until Christmas 1989. When they were visiting their mom, Pat, that Christmas, she learned of a failed suicide that Lynne had attempted. Pat, therefore, refused to return Lynne and Bill, getting custody of both soon thereafter. The judge over custody rights told Pat's lawyer that they were not to go back to Tom and Elaine, but had not filed the papers since it was a holiday. Tom and Elaine tried to have Pat arrested for interfering with a custody order, but the papers were filed before she was actually arrested.

When Tom brought their things to a neutral location (which included an almost new Sears riding lawnmower that belonged to Chris' older sister, Melanie), Chris loaded everything up to be taken to Douglasville. Some of their toys had been broken. Lynne's picture had been ripped in half. Before cranking up the lawnmower, Pat got a mechanic to check it out. Sugar was in the gas tank, but it had not been cranked, so the engine was usable. Also, the motor was rigged in such a way that it would explode if it ever were cranked, killing or seriously injuring whomever tried. Mike was the only one with the mechanical know-how to do this. All of this only confirmed to Chris how much that "family" had surrendered itself to Satan.

Years later, Tom would realize how evil Elaine and her offspring were and divorce her. Eventually he and Pat remarried, and he is on the verge of becoming a full-time evangelist.

Rosalee & T. Christopher Jarrell

CHAPTER ELEVEN

All of this was causing Chris to grow up and take life more seriously. Before this time, he would not read his Bible, but would trust that the pastor was explaining everything correctly. Now, he began to question his beliefs. "What do I really believe?" he asked himself. He began reading the Bible for himself and seeking the truth, as C.S. Lewis, Francis Schaeffer, Josh McDowell, and many others had done[1]. Like them, he discovered that the Bible could be trusted and that the evidence for truth was squarely on the side of the Bible.

Chris entered a literary contest for high school students that was sponsored by Gordon College. He went to the campus and met some of the professors. He would befriend an English professor named Dr. Money when she congratulated him on a first place entry. He thought the campus beautiful, and at her urging, began considering it as a viable option for furthering his studies. He left that day still not knowing that a girl named Rose, who was in her first year there, existed. They would not meet that day.

Auditions were being held for a musical one afternoon at the high school. Chris had never been in anything theatrical. Mr. E. had him teach Physics class once as a prerequisite for passing, and he taught geometry class to eleventh graders once. He also taught computer programming to another class for a week while the teacher was away, but he had never been in front of a lot of adults to do anything. He didn't want to try out, but Chris S. grabbed his arm and dragged him to the auditions.

Ms. S. was the director—a job at which she excelled in addition to teaching English. Ms. R., the music teacher, was also helping, as was student director Susan B..

The play was "South Pacific." Chris didn't know anything about the story, but he did learn that the main character, Emile de Becque, would be romantically involved with another main character, Nellie Forbush. Chris really wanted the part of Emile, especially since it would involve a kissing scene. When he found out that the beautiful Jessalyn would play Nellie, he <u>really</u> wanted the part.

Ms. S. didn't seem to like him as Emile, so she got him to read for several characters. She started laughing when Chris read for the role of Luther Billis, the lead male comedy role. She got him to read this section of the play over and over and changed who read for the people with whom the character was communicating. Each time Chris read it, Ms. S. laughed harder, and a few students would join in.

---

[1] For example, check out "Evidence That Demands A Verdict" (Volume I and II), by Josh McDowell.

"Oh, great," Chris thought to himself, "I'm going to get stuck as this character and I'm not going to get to kiss anybody!" Even in a play, he still couldn't get the girl.

Chris did get that part. The only problem was that Chris lacked any musical talent. Ms. R. told Chris that he had no musical range. She and Ms. S. assigned almost all of the singing parts Chris was supposed to have to other people. He would just do the acting and talking. When all the males would sing together, Chris was told just to mouth the words because his singing could still be heard and sounded terrible. He wasn't even allowed to whistle or hum when the play called for it.

Since his parents had divorced and his dad had kicked him out, Chris had been very bitter and depressed, even having suicidal thoughts. Lacy S., the ten-year-old daughter of Ms. S., had been his almost constant companion and had helped him immensely through his tough times.

Still, Chris had gotten so depressed that he prayed tearfully, "Lord, please bring someone into my life that will love me or just go ahead and take me. I don't want to live anymore. I don't want to be alone. If you want me to live, send a girl to love me, please!"

Around this time, Mrs. A. took a busload of students on a field trip to the Fox theater in Atlanta to see "Les Miserables." Chris kept noticing one gorgeous blond on the bus, and would look at her when he could get away with it.

"I hope I get to sit by her," he told himself. He didn't, but that was fine because his allergies and hay fever acted up so badly that he felt terrible and probably looked worse. He took medicine and the only reason he stayed awake was because the play was so wonderful and powerful.

On the way home, he still kept looking at her. She caught him peeking a couple of times and smiled. He even got up the courage once to say hello. He had never seen her before. The reason why was because she was four years younger than he was, and thus an eighth grader.

She was in the musical with Chris, too. Her name was Cozette and she would be playing the role of Ensign Sue Yeager. One of the main characters in "Les Miserables" had been a girl named Cozette. Chris would sing the love song from "Les Miserables" to himself and think of the Cozette he knew.

"South Pacific" was a huge success. Those in the Drama Club elected Chris as "Best Actor for 1990," though this was the only play Chris had ever been in. Chris hadn't voted because he wasn't in Drama Club. He didn't think he deserved the award. He didn't even think he was that funny. He had just been himself and hadn't even felt nervous. "Oh, no," he thought, "does this mean everyone thinks I'm goofy? Is that the way I really am?"

After the play, a cast party was held at Ms. S.'s house. Even though the play had done well, and Chris had received good reviews by the public and fellow cast members, he was still depressed.

Lacy, who knew Chris' feelings for Cozette, enlisted the aid of Amy L., a tenth grader who had previously tried to help Chris deal with his depression, and who was a friend of Cozette. Somehow, those two got Cozette to come out on the front porch where Chris was sitting alone.

Chris had not been participating in the cast party because he was so depressed. Lacy and Amy also kept everyone else away from the front porch. They had been urging Chris for about a week to ask Cozette to be his girlfriend. They both urged him again just before Cozette came out.

When she came out, she sat on the railing of the front porch beside where Chris was sitting. They talked for the first time and Chris finally summoned the courage to ask her to be his girlfriend. She accepted, but the romance was short-lived.

Since Chris was a Senior and she was an eighth grader, they didn't see each other except when she came into his hall for one or two classes. He would be late for his class just to see her, but since he was an "A" student, the teachers never complained.

Chris and Cozette would also talk before the buses took her home. A couple of times, Chris walked across town to see her at Amy L.'s house. Amy's parents were very nice to Chris and didn't act as if anything were amiss. Cozette lived out in the country, so Chris couldn't go there. He didn't have a car or a license, and it was too far to walk.

Chris wrote a couple of poems for Cozette and read them to her. She seemed to like them. Word spread quickly that the two were "an item." Maybe it spread so fast because of the age difference, maybe because no one had ever known Chris to have a girlfriend before, or maybe because both of them were so nice. Whatever the reason, nobody, not even teachers, objected to the romance, except—her mom.

When she found out that Chris was a senior, she asked him to ride with her and Cozette in her car. She told Chris that he couldn't see Cozette again, nor could he call her again. Chris couldn't understand what the problem was. He was a clean-shaven, "A" student who was in science club, student council, Beta club, and other respectable activities. He was a Christian and a virgin. He didn't have a car or license, so he couldn't possibly take her anywhere, even for a date. He was trying to become Salutatorian, though he wouldn't know if he was until closer to graduation.

Cozette and Chris broke up for about two weeks, and then decided to get back together secretly. This didn't work very well. One day, Chris skipped class to talk to her. They walked out of the building beside the teacher's parking lot and stood in the doorway. They decided they should leave well enough alone.

"May I kiss you this once?" he asked. She said it was okay. Chris looked at her and questioned, "Uh, what am I supposed to do? I've never kissed a girl before."

"You don't <u>know</u>?" she said.

"No, I was hoping you would know," he replied.

They decided just to try anyway, so Chris leaned forward. Just then, the bell rang, meaning she was late for class.

"I've got to go," she said, and then quickly went back in the door, leaving Chris standing there still trying to figure out how to properly pucker his lips. He would never see her again.

He went to his trigonometry class, but sat by himself in the back, though there were only about ten students in the class. The teacher, Mrs. H., asked if he would like to move closer. Chris' bottom lip quivered uncontrollably as he fought with all his might not to cry. Boys don't cry, after all. He just shook his head, unable to speak. She wouldn't call on him again for several days, allowing him to regain control of his emotions.

Amy L. and Lacy assured Chris that everything would be all right and that he would find someone else. Chris was no longer depressed and suicidal.

After graduation, he would write a letter to the editor of the local paper thanking several people. He thanked Mrs. A. for being his closest friend that year and counseling with him. He thanked Ms. S. for opening her home to him so he could finish school in Monticello. He thanked Lacy for "teaching him how to laugh again." He thanked Cozette for "teaching him how to love again."

That last part caused a little bit of a stir, but Chris didn't care. When he needed to feel love again, Cozette had been there, and whether she ever loved him or not, he was thankful for her. When he moved away that summer, he would leave a present for her with some friends of hers, but he never knew if she got it.

He had hoped to take Cozette to the prom, but that was now impossible. He decided to ask a classmate this time, even giving her a gold bracelet. She said yes, but backed out a month before the prom. As a result, Chris decided not to go to his Senior prom, and missed it as he had his Junior one. Though he was disappointed, he was nowhere near as upset as he had been when he had been rejected the year before.

The teacher in charge of the school yearbook that year asked Chris to write a message to those who would still be in school after he graduated. He did and she published it in its entirety. Surrounding the letter were pictures of Chris taken at different times during the year. The letter read:

> My message is a simple one. To all those students who are working their way up to high school: believe in yourself, don't be afraid to try, do your best, and above all, be yourself.
>
> I know the pressures you face. I have faced them and survived. You can also survive. Sometimes you feel that you can never succeed and that you are totally worthless. I have

thought this about myself often. Just don't start believing this. Each of you is worth a great deal.

Don't be afraid to try. Sure, you may not always succeed, but if you do your best, you will feel better about yourself, regardless of whether you succeed or not. I did not always succeed, nor did I always do my best, but when I did do my best, I always felt like I had accomplished something, and that in itself was a satisfaction.

Most importantly, be yourself. Don't succumb to bad influences. It can ruin your life. Once, I allowed myself to be changed by negative pressures. I was bullied and made fun of because of the way I looked and because I liked to do well in school. I listened to the people who considered me a joke. I purposefully began to do badly in school, and did not try. For three years, I was in an intellectual coma. I almost ruined my future beyond repair.

If anything even remotely similar happens to you, don't let yourself be taken in. Don't listen to peer pressure. Drugs, alcohol, tobacco, sex... none of these are necessary to have fun or a good life. It is not impossible to resist the pressures to try these things. Just make up your mind that you will not try them, and if tempted, just say no. It may be hard to say no at first, but it gets easier each time you say it.

If someone calls you "chicken" for not trying drugs and alcohol, just remember that it takes twice as much courage to defend your principles than it does to let yourself be taken in. Don't be a coward. Think of our forefathers, the colonists. It would have been so easy for them to let the British run their lives and succumb to the pressure of the English king, but they decided not to be pushed around and forced to accept their fate. They fought back (and won) and you can, too.

Remember: be yourself, and in time everything will be all right.

Daphne had gotten athletic awards, but since Chris was not into anything that required exercise, he didn't care. When Beta Club awards night came around, he got more awards than anybody, even Daphne, so he felt better at not being able to be Valedictorian. He did make Salutatorian, though.

He was not to be Star Student. Daphne and her boyfriend, Scott, shared that. Chris had hoped to make 1200 on the SAT the first time and increase it each time he took it to make Star Student, but after several times he didn't even break 1200.

Daphne and Scott did. He began to wonder if he was as smart as he had previously thought.

At graduation, he delivered a speech comparing Monticello to the mythical Brigadoon, a place of goodness and peace. When Daphne delivered her speech, she was unable to finish because of her tears. She sat back down beside Chris and a few others, including Michael B., the class president. They were seated beside the podium facing the other students and the parents in the stands.

He wanted to put his arm around Daphne and comfort her. He was irritated with her for getting Valedictorian and Star Student, and considered her his only real rival, but he didn't hate her. He hated to see any girl cry. Still, he didn't move because Scott and he were friends and he didn't want to upset Scott by putting his arm around Scott's girlfriend.

Several people asked him later why he didn't put his arm around her and comfort her. They told him he should have. He has wished ever since he had. She needed comforting them and he did nothing. He really felt like a heel.

Chris had applied to Gordon College and was accepted. He had gotten scholarships large enough to make going there free, so he decided that was where he would go. Over the summer, he lived with his granny in Douglasville and worked at Six Flags.

That fall, he went to Gordon for his first year of college. This would be Rose's second year.

CHAPTER TWELVE

Rose's first year at Gordon went pretty well. She was enjoying her freedom, especially from Jerry. She liked Liz, her roommate, but Liz irritated her, too. Rose had never told Liz what she had been through with Jerry. Liz, not meaning to hurt Rose, but ignorant of Rose's six years of hell, kept asking her if she wanted to have sex with men, to which Rose would reply, "No."

"Don't you want to have wild sex?" Liz would ask. "I do."

"No," Rose would reply. Rose would often wake up in the morning to see a poster of a naked man on the ceiling above her face. Liz had put it there before Rose went to sleep, while Rose showered, but Rose wouldn't see it until the morning. Irritated, she would rip the poster up and throw it in the trash and ask Liz not to put any more up.

"Liz, quit aggravating me and putting pictures of naked men on my ceiling."

"Oh, don't you want to have sex with that man?"

"No, not really."

Liz always had guys around her. She was a regular Scarlett O'Hara. She would whisper to Rose, "I like his body. I think I want to try to date him."

Liz and Rose attended the school dances together. For the second quarter, Liz talked Rose into taking aerobics with her. Liz bought them both outfits. Rose always wore a shirt over her outfit. Liz never did, and she insisted that she and Rose go to the front so everybody could see them. Rose would rather have stayed in back, but she went with her roommate.

"I don't want to have children," Liz confessed. "I worked hard for my body and I don't want to mess it up."

"One day you will. You'll eventually change your mind and want to have children."

Rose got to go home to the Tolberts some weekends. A guy named Kevin gave her rides home. She didn't trust him, but he lived in Douglasville, too, and never tried anything. "He was scary looking," Rose admits.

The Tolberts did come pick her up for Christmas holidays. They took her to the dentist to see about getting the oral surgery for which the childcare organization had promised to pay. He made molds of her mouth and said she could have oral surgery to correct her overbite. They took out the wisdom teeth and set up an appointment for the oral surgery.

They severed the nerves of her upper lip and gums and took out the bone that was protruding. They cut the thin tissue that connected the top lip and the gum, so that she would show gums whenever she smiled from then on.

"That was so horrible—all that pain—and right before Christmas with all that good food and homemade candy. It was hard. That was the only hard thing about it with all that candy and turkey and dressing. Uuuuhhh! I had a hard time chewing it up. I went through it and my mouth was all healed up before I went back to school."

She returned to Gordon, keeping Liz as her roommate. Liz would have guys coming to their window at all hours of the day and night, and Liz didn't care whether she or Rose was even dressed. She would talk to them anyway, so Rose had to be on her guard at all times.

Liz wouldn't go to parties, though. She and Rose would go walking around campus. They would go to the nearby park and swing. They sometimes drove to town, but always attended their classes.

When Rose went back home for Spring Break, the dentist put braces on her teeth. When she returned to Gordon, she met a girl in the game room. The girl asked Rose if she had a boyfriend, to which Rose replied that she didn't. The girl informed Rose that her cousin would be picking her up in a few minutes and asked Rose to meet him.

"But I don't know you," Rose said.

"Well, let me at least introduce you to him." She did and he asked Rose out for a date.

"I don't know," Rose said apprehensively.

"I'll be with you," the girl replied. "You don't have to worry. He won't try anything. I'll go with you."

"What are we going to do?" Rose asked.

"Well, we'll just go out to eat."

"Well, all right. I'll go," Rose said. She sat in back as the boy drove. He took the two girls out to eat, then dropped them off at his aunt and uncle's house while he went to work on his car.

The aunt sat beside Rose and informed her that she was bisexual and was having sex with her husband and the girl that had asked Rose to meet her cousin. Rose was getting a little scared. She had never even met these people before. Rose left and walked to the house down the road where Andy, the boy, was working on his car. She asked him to take her home.

She didn't see him again on a date, though he kept calling her. He asked Rose to go shopping with his sister, which she did. Rose thought Andy was too weird to go out with him again.

A gardener began following Rose around, scaring her. Once, he stepped out from behind a corner, stopping Rose. "I'd like to take you to a lake and have a picnic with you alone," he said. She got away as fast as she could.

That summer, Rose went home, where she attended church a lot. "I received a lot of healing," she reports. "I prayed a lot that the Lord wouldn't let me be branded and X'ed. I didn't want to be X'ed. It seemed that the only people who were attracted to me were men who wanted to have sex with me, or weird men, or psychos."

"Please don't let me find anybody who is crazy or insane anymore or who wants me just for sex," she prayed. Rose would say to herself everyday, "I am not X'ed. I am wonderfully made by the Lord Jesus Christ. I am not marked. I am wonderfully made by the Lord Jesus Christ. I am His creation. He <u>does</u> have someone out there for me who is wonderful and that is a Christian." She was determined that she wasn't going to go out with anybody until the Lord told her that was the person she was going to be with for the rest of her life.

She went swimming some, and baby-sat some of the Tolbert's children. She sat around reading all the Christian romance novels that Grandmother Tolbert owned. "It was a nice change not having to worry about anything and relaxing," she says.

When Rose returned that fall, she had a new roommate because Liz had graduated from Gordon, which was only a two-year school. Rose was the first in the room this time. Her roommate would not come for a few days, and would only stay a month or so before she moved in with someone else.

That first day, Rose sat in her room with the door open playing Christian music. Teresa was wheeling her wheelchair down the hall and heard it. Being a bold person, she came into Rose's room and asked if Rose were a Christian, reporting that she was, too. "I like your music," she told Rose.

"Thank you," Rose replied.

Teresa was born with spina bifada. The doctors said she world never be able to walk, but her mother taught her how to walk as a child by holding chocolate cake out in front of her and making her walk by holding onto bars and figuring it out for herself. She can walk still, though she wears leg braces and uses a walker. Most of the time, though, she uses a wheelchair.

She is a beautiful blond who is very outgoing, talkative, and energetic. She would fly down hills, grab a light post, and change directions at full speed, leaving wheel tracks.

The second day, Rose and Teresa met Kirsten, another beautiful blond. She had lost partial use of her legs because of a reaction to a vaccine around two years of age. She can walk without crutches, but often uses them for long walks. She was as energetic as Teresa, but not as outgoing.

The three of them began hanging out together constantly. Teresa would even move her mattress onto Rose's floor and take up residence. They tried to spend time together whenever possible. They began attending the Baptist Student Union on campus.

They would go to the library to study together. Inevitably, they would end up talking more than studying. "Sometimes, we would actually have to study, but most of the time, we just talked. We would talk about guys and school and how we grew up. Teresa talked about growing up with spina bifada, and Kirsten talked about growing up with her legs not working quite right because of the nerve damage to her legs. I talked about myself some. We all shared a little bit about ourselves with one another. That was interesting.

"I was really happy at this time. I had a real good time. I learned I could be free without having to be wild and having to go to parties and stuff. I could still be a Christian and be free. We also went to the parks some to swing and talk and take walks. We were always doing something—all three of us."

This continued until October. Chris had seen Kirsten several times in the cafeteria. He never noticed with whom she sat. He just thought about how beautiful she was. It didn't matter to him that she was handicapped—she was still beautiful. She was always sitting down at a table with other people, and he wasn't brave enough to approach her in front of a bunch of strangers.

One day, though, he saw her struggling to dip ice cream. She was wearing a sweater and was getting frost all over the front of it. He walked up to her and asked if he could help. She let him, and they began discussing ice cream flavors.

"Do you want any of the peach?" he asked.

"Yuck, I hate peach ice cream," she replied.

"Well, that's down-right un-American," he replied, jokingly. If not un-American, it was certainly un-Georgian. He finished dipping their ice cream and offered to carry hers to her table so she wouldn't drop it or smear it on her crutches. She said he could.

"Wow, she's pretty," Chris kept thinking to himself. He was proud of himself for having the courage to talk to her.

She was sitting at a small table that was just big enough for four. It was located a few feet from the exit of the cafeteria line. Teresa sat to the left and Rose in the middle. Kirsten took the seat to the right, and Chris gave her ice cream to her, smiling the whole time.

He didn't pay much attention to either Teresa or Rose. He was only interested in Kirsten at the time. "I can understand why Chris was attracted to her," Rose says. "She is a beautiful blond with pretty eyes. Plus she was built on top, too, so I can understand."

When Rose saw Chris walk out of the door where the students got their food and into the large area of tables, she heard God say, "That's the man you're going to marry."

"No it's not, either," she argued with God.

"Yes, it is."

"Un-uh!" She didn't want to date anybody at that point. She was enjoying being single and free. "Besides, he's too young!" Chris was barely eighteen and Rose would be twenty-two in a month.

When Chris and Kirsten arrived at the table, Kirsten asked him to sit down. Chris asked Rose and Teresa if that would be okay with them.

"Okay, that'd be fine," Rose said.

"Sure! Sit down!" replied Teresa. Chris sat down across from Rose. He mainly wanted to talk to Kirsten, but Teresa and Rose insisted on asking him questions. He could tell Teresa was a few years older than Kirsten or he. He thought Rose was in her thirties, though she was only four years older than Chris and Kirsten, and only three months different in age from Teresa.

"What's this old person doing here with these younger kids? Isn't she a little old for college?" Chris thought to himself. He didn't realize that many older people, called non-traditional students, attend college. He was not impressed with Rose whatsoever.

The reason Rose looked older than her age is that she had recently gotten a permanent. She had asked for a little wave in her long hair. The beautician mistakenly left the curlers and solution in for the full time, so Rose's hair looked very short because of the tight curls. It was the same style that one of Chris' aunts had always worn, so he thought Rose must be in her early to mid thirties— old to Chris who had turned eighteen the July before coming to Gordon.

Chris felt that they were hounding him with questions. He learned that he and Kirsten were only months apart in age, Chris being the younger. He learned that Teresa and Rose were not that much older than Kirsten and him.

"Where did you go to high school?" one of them asked him.

"In Monticello. From here, take 36 to Jackson and turn right. That will take you to Monticello."

"Where do you live now?"

"In Douglasville with my Granny."

"Oh, really! I live in Douglasville, too," Rose asserted. Chris had not heard of the road off of which she lived, but he knew where Hwy. 5 was, which Rose said led to her house. He reported that he lived down the street from the high school in Douglasville, and Rose said she thought that she knew where that was, but wasn't certain.

"Well, you could take Rose home, then," either Teresa or Kirsten stated.

"I guess so," Chris replied.

"You wouldn't mind?" Rose asked.

"No, I'm going there anyway." Even though Chris was in no way interested in Rose, he wouldn't mind taking her home on weekends and holidays. People had given him plenty of rides over the years, especially since he only recently got his license and a 1979 Oldsmobile Regency. Having company would help him stay awake for the two-hour trip home.

"That would be better than her ride now," one of them said.

"Yeah," Rose agreed, "the guy I ride home with now is kind of hoodlummy looking. He's never tried anything, but he kind of scares me."

"Well, don't worry. I'll take you home whenever you want. I wouldn't want you riding with someone who scares you."

Chris began spending less time with "the guys" from the dorm, and more time with these girls. The girls would talk in the evenings together in Rose's room, as they had been. Now, they talked about Chris in their conversations, too. They thought it was funny that he was hanging around. It was obvious that he liked Kirsten.

"Kirsten," Rose asked, "since he's interested in you, do you think you'll go out on a date with him?"

"I don't know if I'll date him or not. I don't know if he's my type."

"What about you, Teresa?" Rose asked.

"I know he's not my type. What about you?"

"I don't think so," Rose said. She was still refusing to accept that God was saying Chris would be her future husband. She wasn't interested in him at all.

"Well, we can keep him around as a body guard," Teresa said.

"Yeah, he's kind of like a little puppy dog following us around anyway," Rose agreed. They all decided they'd let Chris keep hanging around with them.

Even though the Lord kept assuring Rose that Chris was to be her husband, she wouldn't accept it. "I don't want to date anybody right now," she told Jesus.

She kept watching Chris, though, observing him. She didn't get caught because women excel at this. Chris always got caught looking at Kirsten and the other girls.

"He is sweet," Rose thought to herself. She was watching him again at the dinner table. He looked up at her.

"He has nice eyes, too. What a pretty blue they are!" Chris got up to go to the salad bar a few feet away. Rose watched him as he walked and as he got his salad. "Nice butt!" she thought to herself. She was just starting to let her heart open up, though she still wouldn't accept what the Lord was telling her.

They really wanted Chris to hang around when they found out that he did well in school. He had been hanging around at meals, but had only in the past few days begun spending more time with them. He was now going with them to the library, but didn't know they were talking about him back in the dorm afterwards.

Teresa was having trouble with some math problems and was letting the rest of the people know about it. They had checked out a room with a door and glass walls in the library so that they could talk without getting in trouble.

Chris, seeing that Teresa was struggling, offered to help her. He showed her how to work out the problem, then did it himself to check her answer. After that, she would almost monopolize his time in the library every evening getting him to help her with math. He started helping Rose with her writing and grammar, at which she still struggles. Kirsten usually didn't ask for help, but did occasionally. Chris didn't usually do his homework, partly because he didn't think he needed to do it since he understood it and partly because homework wasn't graded in his classes. It was also partly because he didn't want to do it—

he was a compulsive procrastinator, after all. He enjoyed helping others, though, especially if they were female and cute.

After knowing them a few weeks, Chris asked Kirsten out on a date. "Well, are you gonna go out with him?" Rose asked.

"Yeah, I'll probably go out on one date with him." Kirsten wasn't really interested in Chris.

Rose's heart was beating faster. She wasn't jealous, but she was a little relieved that Kirsten only wanted to go on one date with Chris and that she wasn't really interested in him. Rose didn't understand why she felt relieved, though.

"You know you're going to marry him," Jesus whispered to her.

"Lord, why do I have to marry this man?" she asked. Her heart was beginning to accept it, but her mind would not.

Chris took Kirsten to see 'Memphis Belle' at a theater in Griffin. He didn't know the area, so Kirsten had to give directions to everywhere they went.

"Well, what happened? Where did you go?" asked Rose afterwards.

"We saw a movie," she said.

"What kind? Did you enjoy it? Did y'all have a good time?" Rose asked.

"We saw 'Memphis Belle.' It was good. I had a pretty good time. He had to carry me up some stairs at a park. I thought it was sweet, but I just knew he was going to drop me," she replied. She didn't tell Rose or Teresa that Chris had put his arm around her and shared his coat with her as they sat in a wooden swing at the park.

"I don't know how he did it. I must weigh a ton," Kirsten asserted.

"Kirsten, you don't weigh no ton!" Rose exclaimed. "Well, what did you think of the date?"

"It was fun. I had a good time, but he's just not my type."

"Yeah, but that's okay," Rose replied as she smiled.

"We can keep him around as a friend and as a bodyguard," Kirsten stated. They all agreed to this, especially since he helped them with their homework. He was trying to get a girlfriend. They only wanted free tutoring and a bodyguard.

Chris drove Rose home once or twice. The first time Chris drove up in the Tolbert's yard with Rose, Grandmother and Paw-paw (Chris soon started calling them this, too, as most people do) came out to meet him. Paw-paw was so intimidating that he had scared some people away, even some guys who wanted to date Rose or Lagina. He told some guys not to come back and informed Rose and Lagina that they couldn't see them. Rose always obeyed, not from fear, but because she trusted Paw-paw's judgment.

Chris, however, wasn't frightened of Paw-paw. He knew he hadn't done anything wrong, nor would he, so he didn't feel that he had any reason to be frightened. He did think Paw-paw intimidating, though. Chris shook hands with them and talked for about fifteen minutes, helping Rose get her suitcase out of the trunk.

When Chris drove away, Paw-paw looked at Rose and simply said, "You can see him." She hadn't asked permission, nor did she want to date Chris, but Paw-paw gave his permission anyway. Chris didn't know about this until years later. He was still trying to get Kirsten to like him.

CHAPTER THIRTEEN

"If you see me and Chris by ourselves, please come over. I'm not interested in him, but he still is in me," Kirsten reported.

"Why don't you just tell him?" Rose asked.

"But I don't want to hurt his feelings," she answered.

"I know you don't, but you shouldn't lead him on and let him think you are when you're not," replied Rose.

"You're right. Let me think about what to say to him."

Later, Chris saw Kirsten sitting alone on some steps of a sidewalk on campus. Here was his opportunity to flirt with her unobserved. He sat down beside her and tried to talk to her. Rose saw this and came up behind them to prevent them from being alone, as Kirsten had asked.

Rose started tossing leaves and twigs at Chris, playfully. Annoyed, Chris thought to himself, "I wish she would go away. Dog-gone, she's a nuisance. I want to be alone with Kirsten." He gave her an annoyed look, hoping she would get the message and leave, but Rose wasn't about to leave. Despite her mind's resistance to the idea of dating Chris, her heart was telling her that the Lord was right—she did want to marry Chris.

Chris started tossing leaves and twigs back at Rose. He was easing a bit, not quite so irritated. Kirsten, however, decided to get up and leave, saying her bottom hurt from sitting on the steps too long. Chris and Rose followed.

They walked to Kirsten's car. Kirsten and Chris leaned against her front fender. Rose saw Teresa on another sidewalk, and went to go get her. Kirsten took this opportunity to tell Chris she wasn't interested in him.

"Why? What's wrong?" he asked.

"You're just not my type. You're nice and sweet, but boring. I want someone more exciting."

"Didn't you enjoy our date? What was boring about it?"

"Nothing was really wrong. I'm just not interested in dating right now. Are you upset?" she asked, noticing his frown.

"What do you think?" he asked angrily and sarcastically.

Rose and Teresa walked up and asked Chris what was wrong. "Nothing," was the reply. "I'll see y'all later," he said as he walked off, heading toward his dorm.

"Will you come sit with us tonight for supper?" Teresa asked.

"Yeah. I guess I'll be there," he replied.

As he walked across campus, he talked to himself, fuming. "Boring! I took her to a good movie. She laughed when we talked, and still she thinks I'm boring! Gee, thanks, God. First you send me a girl whose mom hates me, then a girl who thinks I'm boring. Well, that's it! When you make up your mind and decide to send me the woman you want me to marry, then I'll see her, but until then, I'm through trying to find someone!"

After he calmed down, hours later, he prayed, "Lord, please forgive me for losing my temper and getting mad at you. I'll leave it up to you, though. When you want to send me the girl you have planned for me, let me know. Until then, I don't want anyone else. I don't even want to try. It hurts too much."

He did go eat supper with them that night, but left as soon as he finished eating. He didn't talk to Kirsten for several days, and started hanging out with the guys more.

He noticed a large group of guys hanging out at the room across the hall, so went to see what was going on. They were watching a "porno" movie. He stayed for about fifteen minutes, then felt guilty and left.

"Here I am trying to be a Christian and I go in there to watch porno movies. They must think I'm a terrible hypocrite. That's just great!" he said to himself.

From then on, if he went in a room and saw them watching anything with any nudity, he would immediately leave. They began asking him why didn't he stay, so he told them. They said they respected him for it, though they didn't stop watching it themselves.

Chris' anger subsided at being rejected, but he wasn't ready to hang out with the girls as much as he had yet. He decided to try hanging out with the guys and girls equally.

Chris, who was a writer, wrote a poem talking about how a marriage should be pure and holy and open to God, even to the point where Chris said he would only marry a virgin. This upset Rose when he told Teresa, Kirsten, and her one evening at the library.

"Maybe Jerry was right," Rose thought. "Maybe nobody will want me, not even the man God picked out for me." Her hurt quickly turned to anger.

"But what if the girl were raped or molested as a child?" Rose asked, getting louder as her face reddened.

"Well, they couldn't help that," Chris replied. He wondered why Rose was getting so upset. "I'm not talking about that. I'm saying I wouldn't want any woman who had chosen to have sex before marriage. A woman that was raped didn't choose to have sex. It was forced on her. Because she didn't choose it, I wouldn't have any problem with marrying her. In her heart, she is still a virgin because she never gave herself willingly, and would be a virgin if she hadn't been raped. I would consider her a virgin, then, because she didn't do it willingly."

This seemed to calm Rose, but one of the other girls asked, "What about a girl who made a mistake. God forgives them. Why can't you?"

"I can. I didn't say she couldn't repent and get married and be happy. For me, though, I wouldn't want to marry her. I have saved myself for my wife, and I want a woman who has done the same for me." This seemed to appease everyone.

Rose had met a guy at the beginning of the year, before meeting Teresa or Kirsten, at registration. He introduced himself as Joe. He was, like Chris, redheaded and friendly. He was older than Chris, closer to Rose's age, and shorter than Chris, closer to Rose's height.

Rose liked him immediately. She insists she never thought of him as a boyfriend. He gave Rose a teddy bear to remind her of him, and took her roller skating for her birthday, just a short time after she had met Chris. He took her out on his motorcycle. She said she didn't feel guilty about going out with him despite what the Lord was telling her, because she wasn't accepting it. This knowledge, though, seemed to assure her that she couldn't get interested in Joe, so she didn't see any harm in going. Joe said he was interested in another girl, anyway, so they could just go out as friends with no pressure on either.

Chris did not meet Joe until after all this. Chris was sitting in the lobby of the girl's dorm, waiting on the three girls to come out. They came out and saw Chris sitting on the sofa by the entrance, under the windows. Joe walked up and they introduced the two guys to each other. Joe sat down on a desk across from Chris. Rose stood between Joe's legs as they talked. He flirted with her, even giving her a kiss on the cheek.

Chris' blood began to boil. "Wait a minute," he thought to himself, "why am I getting so mad? She's not my girlfriend. I'm not even interested in her."

Rose gave Joe a funny look. "You flirt," she thought to herself. She passed it off as innocent and meaningless, though she didn't move from between his legs. Since she had not been taught any different, she didn't think anything about how this looked. She thought this was just how friends normally behaved. She didn't look at Chris to see what his expression was, even though she knew God wanted her to marry him. It would be a while before she would even consider Chris' feelings.

Chris was furious, though, and didn't understand why. To him, though, it looked like Rose was intimate with a guy he had never met and about whom she had never talked. Chris would not stand that close to someone unless they were "going together," nor would he let a girl get that close to him physically. He was not the type to hang all over girls and flirt. He kept his distance from people, reserving close contact for people for whom he cared. He was not the huggy-wuggy, lovey-dovey, touchy-feely, warm-fuzzy type, though he had written many love poems.

Joe took Rose for a ride on his motorcycle around campus, leaving Chris alone with Teresa and Kirsten. Since Chris was even less talkative than usual, the girls asked him what was wrong.

"Nothing," was all Chris would say. He was glad when Joe left that day, though still not understanding his own anger at seeing Rose and Joe together.

After this, Teresa began telling Rose that she and Chris should get together, though Rose insisted she wasn't interested in Chris.

Rose, still not willing to follow her heart, asked Chris if he would be interested in a date with her foster-sister, Lagina. He and Lagina agreed to consider it if they got to meet each other first. Chris never talked to her on the phone. When Chris took Rose home for Thanksgiving, Rose asked Chris to come to church that Sunday to meet Lagina, which he did. Lagina met him and immediately decided he was too boring for her, too.

Rose enjoyed Thanksgiving, and liked seeing all of the Tolbert's descendants gather together. She says she felt welcomed by everyone, but didn't feel like she fit in. "I wish it was my own family. I never felt like I really belonged. They were nice to me, don't get me wrong. They weren't mean to me. They were always nice to me, but I never felt like I really belonged," Rose insists.

Looking at all the people gathered together, she would think to herself, "Well, this is what it's like to have a real family."

That Sunday evening, Chris returned to pick Rose up and drive back to Gordon. They drove on I-20 toward Atlanta, then on I-285 until it connected to I-75. They exited shortly to go down Highway 19-41 through Jonesboro. This would take them back to Barnesville through Griffin. Jonesboro is considered almost a suburb of Atlanta since it lies just outside of the perimeter made by I-285.

"Let's stop at that gas station and get something to drink," Chris said, to which Rose agreed. Even though Chris had been rejected again, he and Rose were still jovial.

After buying a couple of Cokes, they got back in Chris' 79 Oldsmobile to resume the journey. The only problem was, though, the car wouldn't start. Chris had left his lights on, and, not knowing the battery was old with a few bad cells, it died in the short time they were in the store. They were a little nervous about being stranded at night in Atlanta.

Chris went back in and asked the store clerk to call for a policeman to bring jumper cables, since Chris didn't have any, and nobody else was in the store. Chris and Rose went back out to the car to wait. They were sitting with Chris behind the wheel and Rose against the opposite door, as they usually did.

They were still laughing and joking. Rose decided to lie down across the seat, putting her head in Chris' lap and looking up at the ceiling. Suddenly, things got real quiet! Chris hadn't expected this. Rose smiled and closed her eyes, resting.

When asked years later why she did this, Rose replied, "Because I trusted Chris. He had such a compassionate spirit about him. I wasn't really sleepy. I just did it to be doing it. It felt nice. It felt comforting, and loving, and trusting. It felt nice because his leg was comfortable, and because he didn't try to do anything with me."

Chris looked down at her face. "I never noticed how beautiful she is," he thought to himself. He fought back the urge to run his fingers through her hair and caress her cheek. He held on to the back of the seat tightly with his right hand, and to the steering wheel with his left. He hadn't even been this close to Cozette.

He looked at her hair. The curls had gotten looser, and her hair had gotten longer. The longer it got, and the less curly, the younger she looked. He noticed its color—dark brown, almost black, as were her eyebrows and lashes. He took note of her high cheekbones and olive complexion. He noticed her lips. Everything within him wanted to lean down and kiss those luscious lips, but he dared not. He looked out the window, squeezing the steering wheel and seat harder.

As the police car pulled into the parking lot, Chris told Rose that it had arrived. She sat up and when the policeman got out beside their car, she said, "Wow, he's cute."

Chris, angry again, but not knowing why, said, "Gee, thanks."

"Well, he is."

"I don't care. That's not very nice."

"What?"

"Talking about other guys in front of me and commenting on how good they look. You've never complemented me like that."

"Did I hurt your feelings?"

"Yes," he said. They stopped arguing while the policeman helped get the car started. Once under way, the battle resumed.

They argued almost the whole way back to school. She kept insisting she had done nothing wrong.

"Well, you wouldn't like it if I started talking about girls and how pretty they are in front of you would you?"

"Probably not."

"Well, all right then."

"Jealous!" she said, accusingly (and a little teasingly).

"I am not! And so what if I am! That was still rude!"

"Well, if it hurts your feelings, I won't do it again," she said.

"Thank you," he said, still angry.

Rose kept giggling and teasing him about being jealous. This only made him more angry. After this night, though, Rose would consider Chris' feelings a little more. Their routine didn't change much until they went on Christmas holidays a few days later, around December 7th.

The three girls and Chris decided one afternoon to take a break in the student center in the game room above the cafeteria. Rose and Kirsten went to play table tennis. Chris sat a few feet away in a cushioned armchair. Teresa sat beside the table for a few minutes.

Chris was watching Rose almost the whole time. "Lord, is she the one? She's so pretty and sweet. I like her, but I don't want to be rejected again. I said I'll leave it in Your hands, so I will."

Teresa, perhaps noticing Chris watching Rose, wheeled over to him. "Why don't you ask Rose out?"

"No," he replied.

"Why not?"

"I already went out with Kirsten and she wasn't interested in me. Besides, Rose isn't interested in me."

"Why do you say that?"

"Well, she already tried to set me up with her foster-sister, Lagina, and Lagina agreed with Kirsten that I'm too boring. If Rose were interested in me, she wouldn't have tried to set me up with someone else."

"Well, why don't you ask her out anyway?"

"I don't want to be rejected again."

"But she might say yes."

"And she might say no."

"You won't know until you ask. Don't you like her?"

"Yes."

"Well, why don't you ask her?"

"I just don't want to."

"Just think about it, please."

For a few days, Chris did think about asking her out, then decided against it. He didn't want to be hurt again.

When it was time to leave for Christmas, Chris loaded his stuff in his trunk first, taking about half of the large trunk. He drove over to the girls' dorm to pick up Rose. She finished filling his trunk, and loaded the back seat from floor to ceiling, and back to the rear window. She even put her pillows between them in the front seat. Grandmother had given her all of it since she had come to live with them.

"I've never seen a guy with so much stuff," she said. "I thought guys traveled light."

"What!?! I'm only taking up half of the trunk. That is everything I own. You've taken up the rest of my car, and you've got more at home!"

"Well, they told us not to leave anything in our rooms," she smiled.

They joked and laughed most of the way home. Rose got quiet and silently prayed, "Lord, if I'm going to have any kind of relationship with him, I've got to tell him."

"Chris, I have to tell you something. You know I am a foster child. I used to live in a small town close to Hartwell, called Dewey Rose. I lived with different foster parents than I do now. I lived with them for six years, and he raped me repeatedly. He got me pregnant, and I gave the baby up for adoption." She began telling him her story, filling in a few details, but not all of them. He gripped the steering wheel with both hands, holding on so tight that his fingers and knuckles turned white. She looked out her window as she talked.

His heart was breaking. He wanted to cry, but he wouldn't cry in public. He wanted to beat Jerry up and neuter him. He glanced at her out of the corner of his eye. He wanted to hold her, pet her hair and tell her that she would never have to worry about anyone doing that to her again, but instead, he said to himself, "What are you talking about? Once you drop her off, you won't see her until January. You don't have any relationship with her!"

Rose finished talking in front of a Baptist church, beside which was the road Chris needed to turn down to get to her house. She had wanted to end there so Chris wouldn't feel obligated to be with her or say anything. She wanted to give him time to think about it, and if he was still interested, maybe she had heard from God.

Chris helped her empty her things out of his car, even taking some things inside to her room. Once her things were all out, and Paw-paw and Grandmother were inside, Rose asked Chris to come to church with her Sunday. He said he might, but wasn't sure. The last time he was there, Lagina had rejected him, and he wasn't interested in going back.

"Well, Lord, if he shows up, then I'll try to date him. If not, I guess he couldn't accept what I told him, and I'll just have to find someone else."

Chris had not said anything to Rose, not even trying to comfort her. He was just so shocked by what she told him. Rose insists she wouldn't have let him even if he had tried. "I didn't want him to just feel sorry for me."

Chris left, still not knowing what to say to her. He had no intention of seeing her at all that Christmas. He really wasn't interested in her as a girlfriend.

When he arrived home, his sister, who was also living with their Granny, talked him into going Christmas shopping with her. They looked through the paper for sales. Chris noticed a full page add for a new jewelry store that had opened on Fairburn Road. They were offering necklaces at ridiculously low prices. He asked his sister, Melanie, to go with him and pick out something.

"Even though I'm not interested in her as a girlfriend, I can still get her something as a friend."

They looked at all the gold jewelry, but he didn't see anything he liked. The sales lady informed him they only had a small selection of sterling silver jewelry—about five styles of necklaces. He decided the thick necklaces were too gaudy, so he choose a thin one.

"Will this hold one of those things that hangs off a necklace?"

"A pendant? Oh, yes sir. Even though this necklace is thin, it is strong and will easily hold a pendant."

She showed him a selection of her most popular choices, but he didn't like any of them, not even the heart pendants. "I'm looking for something really special. Do you have anything else?"

"I believe this is it," she replied.

He walked around, looking in each case. He noticed a silver pendant that seemed to be in the wrong place. It was in the shape of a heart, with a hollowed-out center, so that you could see through it. In the center, a tiny, silver rose stood, reaching across the space of the heart outline, from the bottom point of the heart with the stem to the top right of the heart with the bloom. Inside each petal, and etched periodically on the heart, was a patch of silver that shone even more than the rest of the pendant.

"A rose in my heart. That's just what she is. Even if I never date her, this will let her know that she always has a place in my heart. It's perfect!" he said to himself.

"Over here! I found what I was looking for," he called to the saleslady. He had her box it and wrap it. He didn't know when he would give it to Rose. It would probably wait until January. He still wasn't planning to attend church with her on Sunday.

CHAPTER FOURTEEN

When Sunday arrived, however, he woke up earlier than usual and decided to go anyway. He didn't take her present because Christmas was still too far away. The date was only December ninth. He arrived between Sunday School and the morning service.

Rose was dressed modestly in a long dress. "You look nice today," he told her.

"Thanks," she blushed.

They sat on the back pew on the left side. Lagina sat with them, though Chris had rather she not. He did not say anything, though. He doesn't remember any of the service. He wasn't even sure why he was there. He hadn't planned to come that day.

After the service, Rose went to talk to Grandmother. She returned to say that they were going to Dairy Queen and asked if he would like to come, too.

"I guess so," he shrugged. Rose rode with Grandmother since Chris hadn't asked her to ride with him. Chris was a little irritated about riding alone. He had hoped she would ride with him, and assumed she would, but she got in Grandmother's car before he said anything.

Grandmother was also keeping two foster children who were about three years old. They sat with her at Dairy Queen. Neither Chris nor Rose remembers for certain if Lagina was there. If so, she did not sit with Chris and Rose. They got a table to themselves, Rose sitting across from Chris. Rose thought to herself, "It's obvious he's not going to say anything. I guess it's up to me."

When they had almost finished eating, Rose looked at Chris and said, "I sure would like to go see the Christmas lights."

"Yeah, me too," replied Chris, not getting the hint.

"I bet they would be pretty."

"Yeah, they probably are."

"What's wrong with this guy? Is he that clueless? Is this guy going to get this or what? What's his problem?" Rose thought to herself.

"I really would like to go see the Christmas lights," she stated insistently.

Ding!—The light bulb came on! "Oh, you want to go with me!"

Rose sighed, "Yes!"

"Oh, okay. Um, when would you like to go?"

"Whenever."

"Well, I work during the days, and I have to work Saturday night, but the other nights are free. How about tomorrow?"

"That's fine."

"What time?"

"Whenever."

"How about six o'clock?"

"That's good."

Chris was about to burst. He couldn't smile any bigger. Finally, someone was interested in him! This would be his first real date.

The next day, the tenth, Chris was sitting in the living room watching TV with Granny. Melanie walked in and said, "Don't you have a date tonight?"

"Yeah."

"Aren't you supposed to be there at 6?"

"Yeah."

"It's almost 6 now. You'd better hurry up, stud!"

"What !?!" Chris jumped up. "Oh, no! I haven't showered. I haven't picked out anything to wear. I thought it was earlier than that! Oh, no! Oh, no!" He ran around in a panic, finally arriving two hours late for his first date, and without thinking of calling to tell Rose that he would be late.

Rose was sitting in the den, fuming. "I can't believe he's late!" she thought to herself.

When Chris arrived, she acted as if nothing was wrong when he apologized. She didn't let him come in to see Grandmother and Paw-paw, who were waiting beside her, all three watching TV.

Neither Chris nor Rose noticed that his clothes matched her clothes. Chris had on a gray dressy sweatshirt with black stripes and a shield and crest on the pocket. He wore black slacks and loafers. The first thing he noticed about Rose was that she was wearing makeup. She usually didn't wear any, or much.

"Boy, she looks good!" he thought to himself. He still didn't care for her hairstyle, but it was growing out. She had on a thick black and white fuzzy sweater for which he didn't care much, either, but he could overlook it. She wore short black boots. He had never liked boots on women before, but he thought these looked sexy on her.

Rose also wore tight gray jeans. When she turned to tell the Tolberts goodnight and shut the door, her bottom was at Chris' eye level.

"Whuuuu-oooohh!" he thought to himself. "Boy, she looks good in jeans! I never noticed what a cute butt she has!" He quickly looked away before she turned back around and noticed that he was staring.

They got in the car and were finally off. "Where should we go?" Chris asked.

"I don't know. Let's just drive around and see," Rose answered.

They drove around for a few minutes, looking at lights. They entered a large subdivision called Arbor Station, in which neither had been before. Rose sat against the far door, as usual. They were getting confused with saying, "Look at those lights!" and "Look over there!" so Chris started driving slowly and saying, "Left. Right. Left. Right," slowly, and depending upon where a house was that was decorated.

While driving down one of the main streets, Chris decided to try something risky—he put his hand on the seat half way between them, but didn't say anything.

"Oh, please! Oh, please! Please hold my hand!" he thought to himself.

"Hmm. I wonder if he wants me to hold his hand," Rose thought. She placed her hand on his and looked at him. He smiled at her and she at him. Rose felt very content, as did Chris.

After a mile or so, Chris asked, "Do you have to sit way over there?"

"No. Why? Do you want me to scoot closer?"

"Uh-huh," he replied, timidly. She unbuckled her seatbelt and sat in the center, buckling the seatbelt for that spot.

"May I put my arm around you?" he asked.

"Yeah, I guess so," she said aloud. "Sly dog!" she thought to herself. Rose felt happy. She thought Chris was sweet.

Chris did hold her some, but couldn't do it consistently. He had never driven like that before and kept having to put both hands on the wheel for safety.

They got lost in the subdivision. "Have we been that way before?" Chris asked.

"I don't think so," Rose replied.

They would recognize some of the houses and say, "Yes, we have." They would go back the way they came, hoping to get to the exit, but they kept coming to cul-de-sacs.

"Uh! It's another turny-aroundy thing!" Chris would say, not knowing what they were called. After an hour of just trying to get out, Rose was hysterical with laughter. Chris laughed, too, but was concerned that he couldn't seem to figure the place out. He thought about stopping at a house and asking for directions, but since that is against the male instinct, he didn't.

By the time they got out, it was nearly midnight, and they were hungry. He wanted to take her somewhere nice, but those places were all closed. Even the fast food places on Hwy. 5 were closed. He decided to drive to Fairburn Rd. to see if anything was open. The only thing open was Krystal's.

He bought them both several of the little Krystal's hamburgers, fries, and two Cokes. Chris noticed that Rose wasn't eating very well, though she had said she was hungry.

"What's wrong?" he asked.

"I just got my braces adjusted today, and my teeth really hurt. It even hurts to chew."

He picked up one of her French fries and squeezed down the length of it with his fingers, turning it into mush.

"Try it now," he said. "Is that better?"

"Yes, thank you. That doesn't hurt as much." She thought this was incredibly sweet. Nobody had ever done anything so simple, yet so thoughtful for her.

She kept looking at Chris, noticing each feature of his face, especially his eyes. Chris kept looking up at her. He would notice that she was looking back, blush, and look down again. He really wanted to burn her image into his memory so he could think about her even when she wasn't present.

"He's so sweet and innocent," Rose thought to herself, especially when he would blush and look down.

"Why do you keep looking at me?" he asked.

"Because I like to look at you. You have such pretty eyes. Eyes tell you a lot about a person. Why? Am I embarrassing you?"

"Yes. Besides, I want to look at you, but I can't if you're looking at me."

"Why not?"

"It's embarrassing. I just want to watch you, but you keep watching me." After several minutes, Chris decided to look at her even if she looked back. They sat there long after Chris finished his meal, Chris mashing each French fry up for her, and looked into each other's eyes. Rose reached across the table to hold Chris' hand this time. Chris smiled, his heart pounding with love.

Many people today confuse lust and sex for love. That is one reason why the divorce rate is so high. Chris wasn't feeling any sexual attraction toward Rose, and doesn't know if she felt any toward him. What he felt was a sincere love— one that enjoys the other's company no matter what they are doing, and misses each other during times of separation. They could be doing homework together, walking, looking at stars, or anything, as long as they were together.

Chris took her home after one in the morning. Grandmother and Paw-paw had not waited up for her. They trusted her and Chris. Chris walked her to her door, and asked to see her again the next night. They saw each other every night that week. Chris said goodbye, content just to be able to see her again, and overjoyed to have been on a real date! Rose, however, wanted a goodbye kiss, but since Chris didn't offer or ask for one, she didn't try either.

On the sixth night, Chris had to work. He was working at Six Flags. They were trying something new—opening for a short time around Christmas and New Year's. They usually close around Halloween, but they decided to try to get business for the off-season. They decorated the park in white lights and called it "Holiday in the Park."

Most of the rides were closed, supposedly because of the dangers of brake failure in cold weather. The newest ride, The Georgia Cyclone, was the only roller coaster open. This proved to be fatal for the holiday business attempt. There just weren't enough rides open, and the ones that were made people feel like ice cubes in those old metal ice trays.

Chris had asked if he could come over after work, which would be close to midnight. He didn't want to miss talking to Rose before going home to bed. Grandmother said he could come over, even though it would be late.

Chris arrived earlier than expected. Working in the Tram department (trams being the shuttles that take people in and out of the parking lot), he had to wait until the parking lot was empty of guests. Because of the cold weather and not many rides, the parking lot quickly emptied. Douglasville is only twelve miles from Six Flags on I-20, so Chris was at Rose's house in no time.

Grandmother was still awake, watching TV, when Chris arrived. The TV was in the den, which used to be a porch, until Paw-paw put walls on it, converting it into a room. Chris and Rose went to the living room, which was on the other side of the dining room from the den.

They sat down in the dark on the love seat. Its back faced the hallway that led to the bedrooms. They could see the den from there, but not the picture on the TV or any of the people sitting in the den. Rose began telling Chris what had happened to her, giving more details than she had before, allowing him to ask questions. Grandmother went by to go to bed after a few minutes, stopping to give Rose a kiss on the cheek and Chris a hug. She left the dining room light on for them.

Rose laid her head in his lap, having her legs over the arm of the love seat. Chris was horrified by the descriptions Rose gave of her ordeal. He began crying—something he <u>never</u> did in public. He felt that he could open up with her, but no one else. He couldn't imagine why anyone would want to do so much harm to another human being. It hurt even more now that he cared for Rose deeply.

Rose sat up and pulled Chris toward her. She held him and let him cry on her shoulder as she patted him tenderly on the back. She rocked him and told him it was okay. She thought it was so sweet that he was so concerned about her.

"Are you okay?" she asked.

"I don't know," Chris sobbed.

Rose got up and stood in front of him, taking his hands in hers. "It's okay. It's all in the past."

He looked up at her, tears streaming down his cheeks. She couldn't take it any more. She leaned down and kissed him.

He sat there, unmoving, with his eyes wide open in shock. He had never kissed a girl before, and certainly, no girl had ever kissed him before!

"Are you going to kiss me back, or just sit there like a bump on a log?" she asked, smiling.

"I don't know what to do. I've never kissed a girl before." This shocked Rose. She figured most guys had done more than just kiss a girl. This made her happy, though, and made her appreciate Chris more. It made her desire to be with him increase, also.

"Well, for one thing—relax. Don't be so stiff."

"Okay."

She leaned down and kissed him again. He fumbled through it as best he could.

"Is that better?" he asked, hoping.

"A little. You'll get better." She kissed him again, longer this time.

Chris still wasn't sexually attracted to Rose. He wouldn't even think about it until over a year later, closer to their wedding day. He was, however, a mess of emotions. He was at the point of tears from sheer emotion—joyous, frightened, content, and bursting with love—all at the same time.

Rose stood straight up again. Chris leaned forward, placing his cheek against her stomach, and wrapping his arms around her waist.

"Rose, I love you."

A little frightened, she cautiously replied, "Uh, I think I love you, too." She was shocked that someone actually loved her and didn't want her just for sex.

He sat back and took her hands in his. Looking into her eyes, he said, "Rose, I know I love you." He knew that she was the one for whom the Lord had told him to pray, and was glad to have finally found her. He never wanted to be apart from her again.

He stood up and stretched. Rose asked to move over to the sofa. Chris sat down. Rose sat next to him, with her back to Chris, facing the end of the sofa. She leaned back, turning her upper body to face Chris, while stretching her legs along the sofa. They held each other without speaking for several minutes.

He began petting her hair and rubbing his cheek against hers. He placed light, feathery kisses in her hair, on her forehead, on her eyelids, on the tip of her nose, and on her cheeks. He squeezed her tightly in his arms.

"I really do love you, Rose."

"I love you, too."

"Are you sure?"

"Yeah," she replied, nodding her head. Chris still didn't know if she did or not.

"Well, now that we've both said we love each other, what do we do now? I don't know the right words to use. I've seen on TV where guys used to ask girls to be their girlfriends by asking them to "go steady," but that sounds out of date. What am I supposed to say?"

"I don't know."

"I think people just call it 'going together' now, so, uh, will you go with me?"

"Yes," Rose replied. She was so happy that Jerry had been wrong. Someone did want her, and not for sex.

They were now officially boyfriend and girlfriend. It was one o'clock in the morning—the night of December 16, 1990. They were both overflowing with feelings of peace and contentment at finally having each other.

CHAPTER FIFTEEN

Chris got into Six Flags whenever he wanted because he was an employee. He was also given a few free tickets for "Holiday in the Park," so the next night, he took Rose on a date to Six Flags.

Rose wouldn't ride the Georgia Cyclone (or any roller coaster, even if they had been running), so they were even further limited on the rides they could ride. He did talk her into riding the sky buckets, though they went high into the air.

Rose was scared whenever the bucket rolled over the wheels on each tower as they made their way across the park in the air. Chris cautiously and slowly moved from the seat across from Rose to sit beside her and make her feel safer. He would warn her when they were reaching the next tower, since the ride got bumpy over the rollers on top of the towers.

This close proximity, however, allowed for more opportunities for Chris to practice kissing. They rode the ride several times, allowing them time to be alone and cuddly. As other people passed in buckets going in the opposite direction, Rose and Chris got many whoops and whistles.

"That was a 10!" somebody yelled out.

When they got close to the towers, Chris would spell out "B-U-M-P," with a kiss between each letter.

"You like that kissing stuff, huh?" asked Rose.

"Oh, yeah. I wish I knew about this sooner. I'd have kissed you a long time ago."

When they got out, two employees in charge of the ride joked to each other, "I don't know. What do you think? They look pretty high on the guilty scale to me." Rose would turn red and lower her head in embarrassment. Chris would smile extra large and puff out his chest.

They walked to the Monster Plantation. The employee there wouldn't let Chris and Rose have a boat to themselves, so another couple got in the front seat; the middle was empty; and Chris and Rose got the back seat. The other couple was kissing before the boat even entered the building.

"I wish we could have gotten a boat to ourselves," Chris whispered.

"Me, too."

"I don't want to watch them smooch all over each other the whole ride. I would much rather smooch on you instead."

"But not where they can see!"

Chris and Rose looked at the "Monsters" for the first half of the ride. Many of them were dressed in elf and Santa clothes. The kissing booth monster had mistletoe over her booth. When they entered "The Marsh," the part that was dark and scary, Chris and Rose followed the lead of the people in front. They didn't see any monsters in that section.

After the ride was over, they noticed nobody was in line, so they went around and got back in a boat hoping to go alone this time. The employee was about to send them through, but then some kids ran up. Chris and Rose were already sitting in the front. Again, the middle was empty, but the three kids were placed in the rear.

Chris put his arm around Rose, and they leaned toward each other when the ride started. They heard some "Ooohs!" coming from the back seat. Again, they looked at the monsters in the first part. When they were in "The Marsh" section, they hoped it was dark enough to steal a kiss. It wasn't. They heard some more "Ooohs!" and some giggling coming from the back, so they just hugged each other.

Having had enough of the Monster Plantation, they went back to the Sky Buckets. "Y'all must really like this ride," the attendant said as he smiled at them.

Rose was very happy to have a boyfriend. In the back of her mind, she kept wondering, "Will he stay around, though?"

Chris brought Rose to Granny's house for the opening of Christmas presents, when all the aunts, uncles, nieces, nephews, and cousins gathered in one place. This was one of the last Christmases where the whole family would gather together like this. Divorces, anger, and family jealousies would soon splinter the extended family into smaller groups.

Chris' sisters gave Rose some hair bows and necklaces as presents. She thought this was sweet. "They're making me a part of the family already, and these people don't even know me yet," she thought to herself. She was embarrassed that she hadn't gotten anybody anything.

Chris gave Rose the necklace he had bought for her. Her eyes misted as he explained what it meant. She determined to treasure it forever, wearing it every day for several years and causing the silver to turn black with tarnish.

Rose invited Chris to a similar family gathering at the Tolbert's. Rose felt sad because she hadn't gotten Chris anything, and he had given her the necklace. Chris did get some presents, though, just as Rose had. He got several pairs of socks. Rose thought it was funny. "Looks like I got the better end of the deal," she joked.

They couldn't spend New Years together, though. Chris had to work. It turned out to be the busiest night of the whole "Holiday in the Park" trial event. Rose went with the Tolberts and the youth from church to a large Christian music concert called Jubilate. Chris complained the whole night that he was stuck riding a tram in the cold air while his girlfriend was at a concert.

Chris and Rose had not been able to talk to Kirsten and Teresa during the holidays. The news of their relationship came somewhat as a surprise, then.

"Well that's good for you!" replied Kirsten. She was probably relieved to have Chris interested in someone else.

"I knew it. Didn't I tell you, Rose? We talked about it, didn't we, Chris? I knew it!" exclaimed Teresa. From then on, she insisted that she got them together.

All four still hung out together. The only difference now was that Chris and Rose were now boyfriend and girlfriend, and were excessively lovey-dovey. Rose was proud to have a boyfriend and made sure to see a lot more of him.

Gordon had a "Back to School" dance. Rose loved to dance. Chris didn't because he didn't know how, but he went anyway. It was held in the "annex"— an old gym next to campus.

When the time came, Kirsten, Teresa, and Rose came to Chris' dorm to pick him up and drive to the dance. Chris could have walked easily, but Kirsten and Teresa wanted to drive, and insisted on driving Chris and Rose.

"Hey, Chris, there are some girls here to see you," a guy came and told him.

Chris walked out and was amazed. He had seen Rose in full length Sunday dresses for church, and in tight jeans on their first date. This night, Rose wore a knee-length red dress with black stockings and had her hair done up in a style he had never seen her wear before.

"Do you like it?" Rose asked, beaming.

"Wow!" Chris replied.

At the dance, Chris mainly stayed in one corner while Rose and the other two girls danced together in a huddle. They couldn't talk Chris into dancing to the fast songs.

Joe, of whom Chris had gotten so jealous the quarter before, heard that Rose and Chris were dating. He found Rose and asked if he could have one last dance.

"Sure," Rose replied. She considered it just a friendly dance. She didn't ask Chris how he felt. She just told him she was going to dance with Joe and that she'd be back in a few minutes. Chris didn't like it, though. He figured they would just dance to one fast song, not get too close, then come back, so he didn't fuss too much.

They didn't stay right there, though, but walked into the crowd, out of Chris' sight. One fast song ended, and still Rose didn't return. Chris was getting nervous. Wilson Phillips' song called "You're in Love" began playing. Chris didn't know it, but Joe had dedicated it to Rose, asking the DJ to play it as a way to release Rose to go with Chris. He was saying he was happy for Rose and wouldn't interfere with her relationship with Chris.

Chris walked around along the walls on the two sides of the corner where he had been standing. The crowd parted enough for him to see Joe and Rose slow dancing. There was no space between them, and Rose had her head against Joe's shoulder. Chris was instantly furious.

Chris had never been athletic. He never really wanted to be, either. He didn't even like mild exercise, especially any type of running. At that instant, however, he suddenly felt like running full speed down the road where his dorm was located and around campus over and over until he fell down from exhaustion.

"If she'd rather have Joe, then she can have him!" he said to himself. He turned and tried to make his way quickly to the door. Their relationship was over.

Kirsten saw Chris' expression and grabbed his sleeve as he headed for the door. She refused to release it until Chris promised not to leave the dance, but to talk to Rose first.

She found Rose and informed her of the problem. "Chris is very upset with you and you need to come back over there."

"What about?" Rose asked.

"Probably because you danced with Joe."

"It's just an innocent dance."

"I know, but he doesn't think that way."

"Man, men are possessive," Rose thought to herself.

"It's just a dance," Rose kept saying. "I didn't mean anything by it. I promise!" She insisted she didn't want to date Joe, and that he just wanted a last dance as a friend—nothing more.

Rose and Chris left the dance together and walked around campus instead of riding with Kirsten and Teresa. They talked about what had happened. Chris explained to her that to him, close physical contact between a man and woman was a sign of intimacy reserved for a boyfriend and girlfriend, or husband and wife. For her to dance to a fast song with Joe was borderline, but to slow dance and lay her head on his shoulder was a betrayal of their relationship. They had promised to see each other exclusively.

"But it was just an innocent dance!" Rose insisted.

"Do you see me getting close to any other girls? I don't even like to take Teresa's hand when she wants me to hold hers and pull her around campus. Things like hugs, kisses, and holding hands are supposed to be for two people who love each other, not something to do just to be friendly. How would you feel if I hugged and kissed another girl? Wouldn't it upset you?"

"Yes, but I just danced with him. That's it."

"You had your arms around him and his were around you and you had your head on his shoulder. Wouldn't that hurt you if I did that to another girl?"

"Yes. I'm sorry. I didn't mean to hurt you. I didn't think about your feelings. You're right. I see how you misunderstood. I won't do it again. I promise. Will you forgive me?"

"Yes."

They were now under the stair well at the end of the girl's dorm. Rose put her arms around Chris, hugging him tightly. "I'm sorry. I love you so much, Chris. I didn't mean to hurt you."

"I love you, too. I'm sorry I got jealous. I know you didn't know any better and didn't know how I would take it." He lifted her chin so he could look in her eyes—eyes that are sometimes blue, sometimes green, sometimes gray, and sometimes multi-colored with gold speckles in them. His heart pounded. He had never felt so strongly for anyone, except Jesus.

His head dropped suddenly and without warning to give her a kiss that seemed to last as long as the night before Christmas and with more passion and emotion than in all of Hollywood. Rose went totally limp. They both almost fell over because Chris had not expected this reaction from Rose. He caught her, and his balance, and continued the passionate kiss.

When Chris finally raised his head, Rose panted, out of breath. "What's wrong?" Chris asked, worried.

"Ooh, I didn't know you could kiss like that. You learned quick!"

"Why couldn't you stand up?"

"I was shocked! I didn't know you could kiss that well. My legs just stopped working."

Chris felt like Rhett Butler kissing Scarlett O'Hara. "I must be real good," he thought to himself smugly. As did the Grinch's heart, Chris' ego grew three sizes that day. "I'll have to try to get her to do that again someday." To date, though, he hasn't figured out how to bring about the same reaction in her again.

After a few days, Teresa asked them if they had a song that they could call "theirs." Rose and Chris didn't have a song, so Teresa played a song that she heard on a tape. It was by Christian recording artists Billy and Sarah Gaines, and was called "His Love is the Reason." It talked about two people finding each other and becoming friends for the rest of their lives. Their friendship was really God bringing two people together and making them one, as husband and wife. The song fit them perfectly, so they adopted it as their song.

A short time later, Gordon held a Valentine's Day dance. This one was a semi-formal dance. Chris had a suit to wear, but was supposed to find a tie to match Rose's dress. She said it was teal green, but Chris, being neither female nor homosexual, did not understand the subtle differences between shades of the same color that have different names. He thinks he understands mauve now, but still doesn't know what fuchsia is.

"You'll have to show me the dress. Then I can find a match to it."

Instead of just bringing it out on a hanger, Rose tried it on and wore it outside, where Chris was sitting on the bench just outside the doors to the girl's dorm. Her hair wasn't done up fancy. She didn't have make-up or even stockings on, but Chris was speechless just the same.

The skirt and shoulders were made of green satin ruffles. It was sleeveless and open to the bust line. The bodice was made of a black stretch-elastic type of material sown to make tiny bubble shapes all over it. It was meant to hug and shape the woman's frame and features—and it did!

"Do you like it?" Rose asked as she spun around in front of Chris, who was still seated.

"Um... uh... uh-huh," he stammered. His eyes were as big as basketballs, and he dribbled them slowly up and down her frame. He gulped hard.

Rose went back inside to change into her normal clothes. Teresa stayed outside with Chris. "Doesn't that dress look nice on her?" she asked.

"Y... Yes!!" Chris blurted. He was still examining the image of Rose that was branded into his mind.

Rose returned, and Chris was finally able to talk again. "Does teal just mean shiny?" he asked.

"Don't worry about it. Just find a tie to match it," Rose answered.

He couldn't tie a tie, so he had to look for a clip-on. There weren't many green ones, especially shiny green. The only one he found that matched her dress was at the Family Dollar down the street. It was a little short, but if he kept his suit coat buttoned, it wasn't noticeable.

Kirsten liked a certain guy, but Teresa asked him to the dance before Kirsten did. He told Teresa yes. Kirsten, therefore, decided not to go to the dance.

The night of the dance, Chris and Rose decided to meet Teresa and her date at a nice restaurant in Griffin. Rose was absolutely stunning in her teal dress. She had her hair "done up" nicely and had make-up on that flattered her eyes, which drew Chris into them. Her black stockings were set off by a gold ankle bracelet that made Chris' pulse go pitter-patter.

"I'm going to get eyestrain before the night's over," Chris thought to himself.

Chris and Rose sat on one side of the booth, with Teresa and her date on the other side. At the restaurant, Chris ordered fried shrimp (his favorite), and Rose ordered a steak. She poured A-1 all over it before she cut even a single piece off of it. When she attempted to cut it, the whole steak shot off of her plate to her left, and slid down the table, coming to a stop an inch from the edge of the table just over Chris' lap. Rose turned bright red all the way down to her shoulders. The other three laughed hard for a while over the near disaster as Rose quickly put her steak back on her plate and Chris wiped A-1 off the table with his napkin.

Rose felt terrible and looked to be at the point of tears. Chris put his arm around her for a big hug and smile, assuring her that everything was okay. The rest of the meal was uneventful.

At the dance, Chris and Rose had their picture made together. They held each other and slow danced to every song—whether the song was slow or not. He was not about to let anyone else dance with her that night. Rose didn't mind. She enjoyed being close to him.

Around this time, Andy began calling Rose frequently. He threatened to commit suicide if she did not go out with him again. She could not bear the thought of him doing this, thinking it would be her fault.

He came to Gordon and saw the three girls and Chris walking together outside of the girls' dorm. He asked to speak to Rose alone after Rose introduced him. Kirsten and Teresa begged her not to do it, but Chris remained silent. They sat down on the bench beside the entrance to the dorm as Rose and Andy walked to the parking lot and talked.

"So this is the reason we haven't talked?" he asked.

"Yes."

"What about our relationship?"

"I never did want a relationship with you!"

"I think you're a very sweet and kind woman and I really wanted to get to know you."

"It's too late now. You had your chance. Now I've moved on to better things."

"You think you have. I can go and get you a big old ring, fix up a house for you, and make you happy. I'll clean myself up. I promise I'll quit working on my car and spend time with you."

"You had your chance. Now leave me alone!" She walked away.

Chris had been sitting and watching them the whole time. He was upset and mad, but mostly worried for Rose's safety. Kirsten and Teresa had continually assured him everything would be all right.

Andy sent her several presents including flowers and stuffed animals, which Rose threw away. Rose was not interested in Andy. Kirsten, Teresa, and Chris all assured her that she did not need to see Andy again.

"He's a psycho," one girl said.

"Besides, you've got Chris," the other girl added.

"But he says he'll kill himself if I don't."

"Then it wouldn't be your fault. Why give up someone you love just so a crazy person won't kill himself? You will never be happy with him, and what if he decides to hurt you, too?"

"Well what should I do?" she asked.

"Tell him to go ahead, but you don't want to see him and that you already have a boyfriend," one of the girls answered.

The next time he called, Rose told him exactly what the girls instructed her to say. He threatened to kill himself if she didn't go out with him and she said, "Go ahead!" and hung up, though she still worried that he might actually do it.

After that quarter Rose had to leave school because her grades were so bad, especially in English because of her problem with grammar and writing. She accepted it, saying, "I guess the Lord just wanted me here long enough to meet my Chrisyfur." She remained with the Tolberts and worked for a local Day Care center in Douglasville.

Chris drove every Friday night just to see her, then back to school as late as he could Sunday night. He wanted to spend as much time as possible with Rose.

"I thought that it was so sweet that he did that," Rose admits. "He drove all that way just for me. I worried about him, though. I always asked the Lord to protect him and be with him and to put his angels around him and his car until we met again." Chris prayed the same for her.

CHAPTER SIXTEEN

Before Rose left Gordon, she got very upset with Chris because he had signed up to join the Marines the September before they met. Back then, Iraq had just invaded Kuwait and the recruiter was calling Chris almost daily. Chris finally agreed to meet with him, but just to tell the recruiter to leave him alone and to stop calling—BIG mistake.

The recruiter told Chris that if the war lasted any length of time, though it was unlikely to do so, then the draft would start up. If drafted, he assured Chris, then Chris would have no choice but to become an army infantryman and be a "bullet stopper." Chris could not imagine shooting anyone. He could easily die for his country, because he loves America, but he couldn't take anyone else's life in the process.

Chris would rather die as a missionary, telling them about the love of Jesus (as is often the fate of Christians in Muslim countries like Iraq), than as a soldier. "If we defeat them militarily, they will still hate us and be our enemies. If they see the love of God and accept Jesus as their Lord and Savior, then we've won an ally," Chris thought.

"Well, if you join now, you can choose what field you want. To be a chaplain, though, you have to finish college. You can sign up now as a reservist in a non-combat field, then when you finish college, you can make a lateral move to another field and train to become a chaplain."

The recruiter talked about the moral code of the Marines, playing on Chris' faith and beliefs. "Yeah, I've seen the commercials comparing the Marines to medieval knights." Chris' character had been shaped largely by reading many books on knights and chivalry. He had even written a paper in high school that the person with the greatest influence on his life had actually been the legendary King Arthur. Through those stories came a fixed belief that might does not make right, that one must stand up for right no matter what is popular or whatever the opposition, and even if it costs you your life.

The recruiter took advantage of Chris' naiveté and played on those things that he learned from a lengthy discussion with Chris. He had Chris convinced that the Marines were all morally upright individuals.

"But I leave for school tomorrow," Chris said.

"Well, think about it tonight, then come by and sign some papers tomorrow. We'll put you on the Delayed Entry Program, and you won't have to go to boot camp until next summer."

Chris, foolishly, didn't pray about the decision and wait for an answer from God. Instead, he asked relatives what they thought. They all talked about what a good idea it was and how proud they would be of him.

They talked him into joining just as his sister and parents had talked him into trying out for football in ninth grade. Back then, he didn't know the rules of football, nor its purpose. He never did understand what he was supposed to do. He never watched it on TV. He didn't even understand what "downs" were. He was just big and heavy, and people said he would be good at it. He joined, hated it, and quit a month and a half later, but had not learned his lesson. Now he would—listen to God, not necessarily relatives. Only God knows what is best for us. We should listen for His leading.

The next day, Chris stopped by the recruiter's office and signed some papers. He didn't know what he was getting into—only that it would make his relatives proud of him. He didn't even get to see the training videos in the recruiter's office.

Desert Storm would be over before he ever went to boot camp. This was the reason he considered enlisting in the first place, but, of course, the recruiter never told him that he could back out up until taking the oath to defend the Constitution. He thought he had no choice but to go on to boot camp.

Even though Desert Storm was over, Rose was still upset with Chris for enlisting. She was worried that other wars could start up in the next few years and her future husband could be killed and taken from her, leaving her alone for the rest of her life. Even if he weren't killed, she didn't like the thought of him being gone for months at a time as military personnel often are.

Thinking he had no choice, he left with the recruiter after school was out for the year. The recruiter (actually the replacement of the one who had originally talked him into enlisting) took Chris to the Atlanta MEPS, where physicals are given, final paperwork signed, and the oath taken. This recruiter didn't tell him he could back out, either.

Boot camp was the worst experience of Chris' life. For thirteen weeks, he felt as if he were in the pit of hell. His body was constantly tired, his mind exhausted, and his emotions in knots. He was put in charge of saying the prayers for Protestants every night. He counseled other recruits after "lights-out," when the drill instructors went to bed.

He easily saw through the tactics of the drill instructors who were attempting to brainwash him and turn him into a "good" Marine. He saw all around him people turning from their civilian way of thinking to the "correct" Marine Corps way of thinking.

It never did work with Chris. He never saw the Marine Corps as anything great and wonderful, or anything he wanted to do for the rest of his life. He was constantly told by instructors that he wasn't mean or aggressive enough. When other recruits were told this, they acted meaner. Chris, however, took it as a compliment and did not change his behavior. He had no desire to be mean.

He also saw that they were trying to turn each recruit against the rest of the platoon, which is supposedly what would happen in a POW situation. Chris asked permission one night from the senior drill instructor to read out of the Bible and speak in addition to saying the prayers for the night. To his surprise, the senior drill instructor agreed.

Chris read a few verses out of Mark. Then, addressing the recruits and attempting to reveal to them how the drill instructors were trying to turn the recruits against each other, he urged them not to fall for such tactics. He urged them to stick together as a team and a family, not allowing outside forces to dictate their behavior.

To Chris' surprise, the senior drill instructor didn't interrupt or say anything against what Chris had said. When Chris finished, the senior drill instructor just smiled at Chris as if he approved and told him to "hit the rack."

Despite these things, about the only time Chris felt the presence of God was during chapel services on Sunday mornings. The first service of boot camp was mandatory for all recruits, to let them know services were available and how to get to them, but the rest were voluntary. Chris often went alone, or with one or two others. He once had four go with him, but never more.

The other recruits would spend the time writing home, shining boots, or cleaning rifles. They often tried to persuade Chris to stay in the barracks and do the same thing. He wrote letters after lights-out by flashlight under the covers, writing letters to Rose almost daily. His boots and rifle would have to wait and were never as shiny as any other recruit's.

He attended services every chance he got, which was only on Sunday mornings. Only once or twice did the drill instructors make him stay in the barracks instead of going to services. They called him names like "Preacher Boy" and "Oral Roberts," trying to make fun of him and discourage him, but it had the opposite effect on Chris. This is illustrated in a letter that Chris wrote to Rose dated July 28, 1991:

My Beloved,

How are you? I miss you extremely. I haven't received a letter from you in several days, nor even a birthday card. I'm worried. I know you're being faithful and God is watching over you, but I need to hear from you. I miss you so much. I keep thinking about you, how you look, your face, how much I want to hold you, how much I want to marry you and live happily with you forever. I keep thinking about home and all the things I used to do. I miss everything. I'm very homesick. I wish I were through this and back to you. Your Love for me keeps me going. I know I can make it with God's help and your Love.

Yesterday was my birthday. I got about 7 letters (cards) from Melanie, Mom, Granny,.... Melanie sent pictures from my going away party. I hope you've seen them. You look so beautiful! Senior Drill Instructor Sgt. H. looked at them and asked who you were. He couldn't believe I had a girlfriend. He said you looked 16, not 22. Everybody keeps joking with me about being a virgin and waiting until we are wed to have sex. It makes me feel good that we decided not to have premarital sex and have kept that promise. The jokes don't bother me at all. I know we are doing what God wants, so I'm happy.

One drill instructor asked Chris one evening if he planned to become a chaplain someday. Chris replied that he did, to which the drill instructor replied that it was a good idea. This was the same drill instructor that made fun of Chris the most and called him names most often.

When running, Chris would run on the edge of the pavement, hoping to slip and break an ankle and be sent home. He never did. He heard that a recruit in another platoon had put both legs between the frame and mattress of his rack (the military term for bed) and pushed off backwards with all his might, breaking both legs in an attempt to get sent home. Chris considered this, but never tried it.

Chris almost lost hope while there. He could feel the presence of evil constantly at boot camp. One morning while in formation awaiting drill practice, Chris, at the point of despair, glanced up to see a blue-jay on a power line a few feet above him. It looked directly at Chris and started singing, then flew away. He realized the Holy Spirit was speaking to him that even on Parris Island, which seemed to be Satan's throne, God was still there to comfort and strengthen His People. This made Chris feel better.

One of the songs sung at church services that helped Chris through this time was the old spiritual, "Swing Low, Sweet Chariot." He would sing this to himself over and over everyday, longing for the angels to "carry [him] home"— either back to Rose or to heaven. He read the Christmas story recorded in the second chapter of Luke in the Bible many times, being comforted that God loved him so much that He became a human and died for us that we would have the *opportunity* to go to heaven.

A verse that Chris said to himself over and over for strength and comfort (especially during PT—Physical Training), was Isaiah 40:31. It reads, "But they that wait upon the LORD shall renew their strength; they shall mount up with wings as eagles; they shall run, and not be weary; and they shall walk, and not faint."

Two-thirds of the way through boot camp, the recruits were taken to the rifle range for two weeks to practice shooting at targets from various distances. Chris had no problem shooting at paper targets, but couldn't stand the thought of actually shooting a person. He was more depressed than usual.

One day, while in the bathroom, or "head," with the other recruits just before lunch, Chris started crying uncontrollably. One of the other recruits ran to get a drill instructor, who came quickly.

"Why are you crying?" the drill instructor asked.

"This recruit doesn't know, sir," Chris replied. Recruits were not allowed to refer to themselves in the first person, or to anyone else in the second person. They were only allowed to speak in the third person, which is why Chris answered with "this recruit" instead of "I."

"Did another recruit hit you or say anything to you?" he asked.

"No, sir. No recruit said or did anything to this recruit."

"Did you fall or get hurt?"

"No, sir."

"Can you stop crying?" This was the first time Chris had seen any of the drill instructors act sincerely concerned about any of the recruits. It surprised him.

"This recruit is trying," he replied, sniffing between words. This made him cry harder. He was getting really embarrassed, but did not know why he was crying.

The drill instructor took Chris to the senior drill instructor for the platoon, who talked with Chris privately. After a lengthy conversation, most of which Chris is unable to remember, the senior drill instructor learned of Chris' plans to become a chaplain.

"Your recruiter really took advantage of you. The Marine Corps doesn't even have any chaplains!"

"It doesn't?" Chris asked in surprise.

"No. We are the smallest branch of the military. We started out as a sub-branch of the Navy, so the Navy takes care of all of our chaplain services. They take care of all of our medical and dental services, too. I'm afraid you signed up with the wrong branch to do that. I'll schedule an appointment with the chaplain for you and you can talk it over with him."

Later, Chris did get to see the chaplain. This man, who seemed so nice and concerned during church services, was very mean and verbally abusive to Chris in the office, accusing Chris of trying to use religion to get out of his duty, for which Chris had volunteered. The Chaplain wouldn't listen to what Chris had to say about being tricked by the recruiter. Chris did want out of the Marines, but he had never wanted in, either. Meeting the chaplain, then, did no good.

The recruits were taken into a gas chamber toward the end of boot camp and made to take off their gas masks for several minutes. Chris put his nose and mouth inside his biological/chemical warfare suit to breath, but since there wasn't an airtight seal, he still breathed in some of the vapors. This caused him to develop asthma.

It didn't give him asthma, because he had inherited it from his father. His father had asthmatic symptoms until he turned twenty-one, then never had any more. Chris had never had symptoms until after taken into the gas chamber at Parris Island. It didn't get bad until the second time he was exposed to the vapors, at a gas chamber recertification. Only after this second time did a civilian doctor diagnose him with asthma, which has only gotten worse over the years. The doctor was the one who told him that the gas chamber could not give Chris asthma, but could have triggered it so that it showed up at that time.

Since Rose was ashamed of her lack of writing skills, she wrote letters to Chris only once or twice a week, whereas Chris wrote almost daily. Rose did miss Chris terribly. In a letter dated September 3, 1991, she wrote:

> My love of my life,
> Hello! Again. We have 9 more days including today until the day comes when I can see you again. I feel sorry for Melanie because I am riding with her down there to see you. She will most likely get tired of me telling her I can't believe we are really going to get to Chris at last. One week and 3 days to go until we are together again. I love you!...
> Last night as I was going to bed I was looking at your picture like I usually do before I go to bed and I started crying. I missed you so bad. I knelt down on the floor and held your picture close to my heart and told you I love you Chris. You have worked yourself into my life to stay permanently. I started thanking the Lord for bringing you into my life. You are so handsome to me. You are the sweetest, gentlest, most loving, kindest, most innocent person and I thank my Lord and Savior Jesus Christ for blessing me with you. I felt better after I cried and talked to God. I went straight to sleep when I got in bed with no worries on my heart.
> I love you more and more each day so you better watch out. I will never let you go without a fight to any other woman. I will hold on to you with all my love and all I have.
> Teresa is right when she said it would crush me if you ever left me because I am so much in love with you, so please don't ever leave me Chris. I love you too much to go on without you.
> I told Melanie I missed you more in the last couple of days than the whole summer. Like today I kept calling everyone Chris besides their right names, even the girls. Now that's bad. I have been thinking about you a lot. I think I miss you so much because I am ready for you to come home. I have waited long enough and it is getting closer to you getting out of boot camp and I can see you again. I want to see you so much to tell you I love you in person.

He was very glad, then, to be able to see Rose again when boot camp was over.

He now detested the Marine Corps for its deceit in recruiting, its lack of morality (despite what the commercials lead one to believe), and for taking him away from his family and friends. He still supports the troops themselves and prays for them, but can in no way condone the immorality that is openly practiced in the military.

For the next few years, Chris would get physically sick every time it was time to return for duty. He would also be emotionally on edge and grumpy/angry until days after he returned home.

It did him no good to hear over and again from various enlisted and officers how proud they were to cheat on their girlfriends and wives every time they came to drill on weekends. He loathed to listen to tales of drunkenness and immorality. He also terribly missed Rose, not wanting to be away from her again for any length of time.

The next few years with the Marine Corps were pleasant for neither Chris nor Rose, who felt the same as Chris did about the military. They considered every minute Chris would spend with the Marines as wasted time. They believe joining the Marines was the biggest and worst mistake that Chris had ever made.

Years later, when Chris was finally taken off active reserves and placed on inactive reserves, his platoon sergeant told him, "You are a good Christian, but you are a sorry Marine."

Chris could only say, "Thank you."

Rosalee & T. Christopher Jarrell

CHAPTER SEVENTEEN

Since Rose had remained faithful to Chris the whole time he was away at boot camp, Chris was even more determined to marry her. When men would try to flirt with her at church while Chris was away, she would sit close to Grandmother and Paw-paw.

Paw-paw, as usual, intimidated guys into leaving Rose alone, just by his presence.

She would not have a driver's license until years later, so she could not drive anywhere for anyone to flirt with her. Grandmother drove her to work everyday, and picked her up, too. Still, the fact that she <u>chose</u> to remain faithful to him really impressed Chris.

From college, Chris wrote to Rose:

11-18-91

My Dearest,

How are you, my love?... I love you. It's two days after our 11-month anniversary. That means it's less than a month until our 1-year anniversary. 1 year! Did you ever think that you would find someone to love for that long and know that you would spend eternity with that person as husband and wife? I prayed for it for five years. Then you came to fill the emptiness in my heart and to give me the love I needed so desperately. Thank you for loving me, my wife. I love you, my little Rose. I love you.

Soon, I pray that God will allow us to be wed. I pray for that several times daily. It is the strongest desire in my heart. I want to be your husband more than I want anything else on this earth. I want to be with you, sleep with you, make love to you, hold you, touch you, kiss you, eat with you, worship God with you, do His ministry with you, have children with you, live for all eternity with you, grow old with you, greet God in heaven with you, do everything with you. Rose, I want to marry you. I want to love you. I do love you. I love you, Rose. I Love You!!!

Does it feel as good to you when I say "I love you" as it does to me when you say "I love you" to me? Does your heart beat faster? Do you feel a warmth in your chest, above your heart, that spreads out over your body and makes your skin tingle with energy? Do bad thoughts and feelings disappear when you hear those 3 words? Do you feel happy, excited, loved, needed, desired, peaceful, and not alone? Do you know that I do love you? Do you realize how much I do love you? Do you know that everything I do is for you and my every thought concerns you? Do you know that I am devoted to you alone? Do you know my heartbeats the words "I Love You, Rose" every time it pounds in my chest? Do you know that I am yours, totally? Do you know that I trust you more than I trust anyone, even myself? Do you know that my love for you is unending, undying, unquestioning, and unconditional? Do you know that I love you more than I love my own life? Do you know these things, Rose? Do you know that I love you?

Even though he wanted to ask her to marry him, he didn't see any way to afford an engagement ring on his small salary. He was working part-time and attending college, too. At church, he would often write notes to her saying, "This is unofficial, but if I <u>were</u> to ask you to marry me, would you say yes?"

She would write back, "Yes," but she knew he couldn't afford a ring. She knew he wouldn't ask her officially until he could buy one.

He secretly found a ring that was both beautiful and low priced. He bought it, then made plans to surprise her. Their one-year anniversary of being boyfriend and girlfriend would be coming up in a few months, which would make a perfect time to ask her to marry him. Thanksgiving, Christmas, and Valentine's Day had been options, but their anniversary was something special to them alone. The other days were holidays for everyone. He kept the ring in his desk at the dorm until it was time to ask her.

On returning to school after spending summer at boot camp, Chris discovered that the girls' dorm was now the guys' dorm, and what had been his dorm (a coed dorm divided into guys' and girls' wings), was now the girls' dorm exclusively. It was newer and nicer, so the administration wanted the girls to live there (girls would take care of it better, as the previous year showed). Guys, after all, are known for living in filth, especially as bachelors, so the old dorm would be perfect for them, too, thought the administration.

To Chris' surprise, he was assigned the room that had been Rose's the year before, and even chose the same bunk, though he wouldn't realize it until Rose told him that was the one in which she had slept. Chris, being the romantic person that he was, loved it.

He continued his boot camp practice of writing to Rose almost daily, even addressing the letters to Mrs. Rosalee Jarrell, though they weren't even engaged yet. He would write all over the back of the envelope sweet names like "My Beloved" and "My Little Rose."

Rose would write back in similar fashion, saying that she would be glad when she was really Mrs. Thomas Christopher Jarrell. She would write on the envelope names like "My Puppy Dog" and "My Teddy Bear."

Chris would sit at his desk staring at all the pictures of Rose that he had, which covered the area around his desk. He would write love poems, which he submitted to the Literary Magazine, of which he was Assistant Editor. All of this earned him the nickname "Mr. Mush" from the guys in the dorm.

Sticking with the idea of asking Rose on their one year anniversary, Chris decided to do some of the same things that they had done the year before, adding a few different elements. He even wanted to ask her to marry him at the exact time he had asked her to be his girlfriend the year before—1 a.m. the night of December 16.

Chris asked Rose to dress up for their anniversary date. She wore a dark colored knee-length dress with pink, red, and blue flowers and black trim. He wore a dark colored suit. They went to see the Christmas lights as they had the year before, though Chris didn't get lost this time. As a result, they got tired of doing this after about an hour.

Chris drove to Red Lobster to treat Rose to a fancy meal, instead of the after-midnight Krystal's from their first date. Realizing that he had not brought enough money to pay for their meal, Chris asked Rose to wait there while he ran to an ATM. Embarrassingly, this took about thirty minutes. When he walked back into Red Lobster, and before he went to his table, he asked his waitress to bring out the surprises that he had left there that afternoon.

She brought out a large flower arrangement and a big present. Rose read the card on the flowers first, then Chris explained the meaning of the different flowers in the arrangement that he had asked the florist to create.

"The twelve red roses are for the year that we have been together—one for each month," he explained. "The three white carnations are for God (the Father), Jesus, and the Holy Spirit, who brought us together. The two pink carnations are for us apart, and the one red carnation is for us together."

Then, Rose slowly opened the large box. Inside was an old blue toy koala. It was Chris' from when he was "growing up." He had left it at Ms. S.'s house with Lacy until he found the woman he was to marry. He didn't want to take it to college with him because he might get embarrassed from the teasing of the other guys. He had gone back to Monticello a few days before their anniversary in order to retrieve it.

Chris had told Rose the story of the koala, called "Pookie," and that he would give it to the woman he planned to marry, but she had never seen it before. When she opened the box, she just stared at the worn toy. She didn't say anything, so Chris wondered if she understood what it meant.

"Do you know what that is?" he asked.

"It's Pookie!" she said, clutching it to her chest as her eyes misted.

He didn't "pop the question" right then, wanting to wait until 1 a.m.. Since they still had plenty of time, and not wanting to look at more Christmas lights, they decided to go to Blockbuster and rent a few videos—the "Grinch," "Frosty," and "Santa Claus."

They only had time to watch the Grinch, which they did at Chris' house, where he was living with his granny and his sister, Melanie. Melanie would be getting off of work at midnight, and would be home a few minutes after that. She knew that Chris was planning to propose to Rose that night, though she didn't know how he planned to do it. Chris didn't want Melanie to spoil the surprise by asking if he had yet, so he took Rose for a ride to look at more Christmas lights.

A few minutes before he planned to be there, he asked Rose to close her eyes, not telling her where they were going. He drove to the church, pulling directly in front of the entrance. He asked her to open her eyes.

"What are we doing at church?" she asked, bewildered.

"I thought it would be appropriate to spend our one-year anniversary in prayer, thanking God for the year He has given us."

"Oh, okay."

"Will you go check the door and see if it's unlocked?" he asked, knowing it wouldn't be. While her back was turned, he quickly reached into the glove compartment and took out the keys and the ring. He had gotten the keys (and the pastor's permission) earlier that day. He had left the ring in the glove compartment because he didn't want her to feel it in his coat pocket when they hugged. He was also concerned that the box might get crushed or fall out if he put it in his trouser pocket.

"It's locked," Rose reported.

Getting out of the car, Chris answered, "That's okay, I have the key."

They walked down to the altar steps just in front of the pulpit and knelt down. Chris allowed Rose to go first. He knelt on one knee, planning to ask her when he finished his prayer. Their prayers, however, were longer than he expected. His one knee got tired, so he knelt on both knees.

He thanked God for the year they had been together, and for bringing them together. As he pulled the ring out of his pocket, he said, "Lord, please bless what I'm about to do."

Rose opened her eyes, wondering what <u>was</u> he about to do?

"Rose, will you marry me?" he asked, holding up the tiny hatbox shaped box that was designed to look like a small Christmas present. Before he could open it, she tackled him.

If he had been on one knee, he could have rolled to one side when tackled, and would have either been on his side or his back, but comfortable. Being on both knees, though, he fell back with his legs folded under him, which was rather painful. Not only did his own weight push down on his legs, but Rose was on top of him, too.

She had her arms around his neck, moving them side-to-side. Chris felt like she was trying to rip his head off. Rose was nearly hysterical.

She finally let him up, but she was shaking and breathing rapidly. Her face and neck were all red from excitement.

"Well, aren't you going to open it?" he asked.

She put her hands out to try, but she was shaking too much. "You open it!"

Opening the lid, Chris asked again, "Will you marry me?"

She tackled him again. He had not gotten off two knees, so his legs were folded under him again. She shook his neck again, too.

When she finally let him up, he asked, "Does this mean yes?"

Nodding her head rapidly while out of breath, she exclaimed, "Yes!"

Sliding the ring on her finger, he asked once more, calling her name as if they were already married, "Rosalee Jarrell, will you marry me?"

"Yes, Thomas Christopher Jarrell. I will marry you," she said through tears. She went to hug him again, but Chris put his arm out behind him to keep her from tackling him. As she hugged him, this time without trying to dislocate vertebrae, he moved his legs around into a sitting position.

"Did I surprise you?" he asked.

"Yes! You said you didn't have any money to buy a ring, and that we would have to wait."

"Do you like it?"

"It's beautiful." It was gold with several small diamonds embedded around the sides with a larger diamond in the center.

"So are you. I love you, Rosalee Jarrell." They sat there on the floor in front of the altar for a long time, holding each other and crying tears of joy.

"Thank you, Jesus," Chris whispered.

Rose and Chris were beaming for the next few weeks. They would tell everyone they knew, including the bank tellers in Kroger's on Highway 5 and in the one on Fairburn Road. Then Rose would show them the ring for everyone to "Oooh" and "Aahhh."

Chris and Rose decided to get baptized together the next time their church held a baptismal service. Both had been baptized previously when they accepted Jesus as their Lord and Savior. Chris would not have any relationship with his dad for several years, so he didn't worry what his dad thought. His mom, however, was totally against it.

Chris had been baptized earlier in a Baptist church, of which denomination she is still a member. Chris, however, had become Pentecostal since meeting Rose, though he had agreed with the Pentecostal doctrine while still a Baptist. His mom thought he was getting rebaptized because of this change in denomination, and was against it since she has never cared for Pentecostal churches anyway.

This was not the motivation that Chris had, though. The baptism that he had when he accepted Jesus as Lord and Savior was, according to the Bible, an outward sign of his belief and acceptance of Jesus' death on the cross as sufficient and necessary for Chris to be forgiven for his sins. That is done on an individual basis—each individual must do this <u>after</u> conversion as a sign of his or her faith. It is merely a sign. Baptism doesn't save a person. Only Jesus' death (in our place) on the cross and our acceptance of it by faith can save us.

Since baptism is only a <u>sign</u> of faith, Chris wanted to show that "As for me and my house, we will serve the Lord." He wanted to show everyone that he and Rose and their family would be dedicated to serving God. This, then, was Chris' motivation for Rose and him to get rebaptized. Rose agreed with his reasoning.

Rose was excited that God's promise to her would soon be fulfilled. Before the wedding, however, Rose was starting to get nervous and anxious. Noticing this, Chris asked her what was wrong. "I'm just nervous. It's nothing," she said.

Inferring about what she was nervous, he asked, "Are you still worrying that you won't be able to satisfy me sexually?"

"Yes," she admitted, lowering her head in shame. "Jerry said the reason he did stuff to me was because Linda no longer satisfied him because she had had children and those muscles were loose. You know I've already had one child. What if I don't satisfy you?"

Chris, attempting to ease her fears, put his hand under her chin, raising her head to look in her eyes. "Rose, I love you. My love is more than just a warm feeling. Love is not a feeling, it is a commitment and a decision. I <u>choose</u> to love you, no matter what. It doesn't matter to me whether your muscles are loose or tight. That's not why I'm marrying you. I'm marrying you because I want to be with you every day for the rest of our lives. I am committed to you.

"If love were based on feeling or what the other person does, then I could say I don't love you the first argument we had. Love, how it's supposed to be, and like the Bible talks about, is a commitment and decision that remains in effect even when there is no feeling. After all, God loved us even when we didn't love him. Jesus loved us enough to die for us even though we are sinners. God's love, true love, is unconditional.

"Rose, my love for you is unconditional. I love you because you are you and I want to be with you, always. I love you because God gave you to me, and me to you. You are the greatest blessing to me besides my salvation. You are the best present the Lord has given me besides my salvation. Rosalee Jarrell, I Love You."

The wedding seemed to them to be taking an eternity to arrive. They were still calling each other Mr. and Mrs. Thomas Christopher Jarrell, even though they had not been married yet. Sadly, Satan used this opportunity to deceive Chris and Rose. One night, while they were alone (which two people who love God and each other should never do, anyway) Chris became very upset.

"What's wrong, Chris?" Rose asked, concerned.

"We keep calling each other husband and wife, but we aren't. I still have to leave you every night. Officially we are still single. I can't be with you all the time. We can't even do what husbands and wives do [Chris meant sex]."

"Wait just a little longer," Rose pleaded.

It was then Satan gave Chris a lie to which he listened. "Well, God married Adam and Eve. They didn't have any preacher to perform a wedding. If we were stranded on a desert island, we would only have God to marry us. Why can't we just go ahead and say our vows to each other?" The problem is that Chris and Rose were not Adam and Eve, neither were they stranded on a desert island. They had a preacher. This false reasoning, which came from Satan, was invalid. Had they been more knowledgeable about the Bible and the tactics of Satan, they never would have fallen for this lie.

"But what about the wedding? I still want a wedding. And what about our families? They want to come to it, too."

"We can still have the wedding. I don't want to disappoint everyone. I just want to be husband and wife in reality." What Chris really wanted, though he wouldn't admit it, was sex.

"Okay. I guess that will be all right."

They knelt down and recited their vows to each other and prayed. Against their better judgment, they then consummated the relationship. Afterwards, Rose not only worried that she wouldn't be able to satisfy Chris sexually over the years, but she now worried that Chris was only after her body, just like other men. She worried that since she had given herself to him, he would leave her, having gotten what he wanted. Chris had unknowingly betrayed the ones he loved most—God and Rose. He had seriously damaged their trust in him. Had he realized this, he would not have done it, but he was not thinking with his mind and logic. He made the decision based on emotion and feeling, and it was the wrong decision, as premarital sex always is.

Rose and Chris, like Adam and Eve, really felt guilty afterwards. They thought about it and prayed for several weeks. When they talked about it again, they agreed that what they had done was sin. They prayed together and asked for forgiveness. Then, they agreed to wait till the honeymoon before doing anything else sexually.

"I don't want our honeymoon to be meaningless. If we keep going, when we do have our honeymoon, there won't be anything new and exciting. The honeymoon is supposed to be the time when we bond together emotionally, physically, and spiritually. I don't want to spoil that time. I love you too much," Rose pleaded.

In recent years, Chris has talked to some men that went golfing and did other things on their honeymoons instead of bonding with their new wives. They said that they had been having sex before marriage, so it was nothing new. Instead of being with their wives during this important time, they selfishly did their own things. That is what sin is: putting self before anyone else. When Chris listened to Satan and persuaded Rose to have premarital sex, he did it because of selfishness. He didn't care about what was right or what was best for Rose or their relationship. Jerry did the same thing. He raped Rose because of his selfishness, not caring what was best for Rose, his wife, his family, or his soul.

"You're right, Rose. I'm sorry I talked you into doing what we both knew to be wrong. That is just what Eve did with the apple. I guess if I had been in the Garden of Eden, I wouldn't have done any better than Adam and Eve. I'm sorry, Rose. Please forgive me. I am willing to wait till our honeymoon. I love you enough to wait, and put our relationship above what I want."

CHAPTER EIGHTEEN

Chris and Rose chose for their wedding day June 2, 1992. This had been the anniversary of Chris' granny and granddaddy. His granddaddy died of emphysema. He was in the hospital a while before he passed away. Though not expected to live until their fiftieth wedding anniversary, he hung on to life until his wife arrived at the hospital the day of their anniversary. He told her that he loved her just before passing away.

Chris and Rose thought that this day would be perfect, then, for them to exchange their vows, since it had already been shown to be a day of true love. Like the field of Gettysburg, this day had been somehow hallowed by death. They could think of no better day, and hoped for as happy a marriage as his grandparents had had.

Chris and Rose picked out the wedding rings together, shopping at some large Atlanta jewelry stores, and smaller ones in malls and shopping centers around Atlanta. They finally found the perfect rings at a store right there in Douglasville, on Broad Street. They were excellently priced and allowed Chris and Rose to engrave more on the insides of their rings than anyone else. Chris had "Rose & Chris June 2, 1992" engraved in his, and Rose had "Chris & Rose June 2, 1992" engraved in her ring.

They shopped at several wedding boutiques and formalwear shops before finally finding a dress for Rose that they could afford at a J. C. Penny Outlet store. The dress was long-sleeved with a high, Victorian-style collar. It was accented with a few faux pearls. The back was cut out in the shape of a heart.

Since they were paying for the wedding themselves, they decided to let Chris and the groomsmen just dress in their best Sunday suits, and the bridesmaids in their best Sunday dresses. Mrs. A. helped Chris to design his own wedding invitations on a computer. It had a laser printer that did high-quality printing. Chris bought high-quality paper on which to print the invitations. They read:

> For this cause shall a man
> leave father and mother,
> and shall cleave to his wife:
> and they two shall be one flesh.
> —Matthew 19:5

> Two hearts, one love;
> Two rings, one promise;
> Two people, one life;
> Two eternities, no regrets.
> —T. Christopher Jarrell

Thomas Christopher Jarrell
and
Rosalee Hand
request the honor
of your presence
at their wedding,
June 2, 1992,
7:30 p.m.
at
Soul's Arbor Tabernacle,
Douglasville, Georgia.

Reception to be held in the
fellowship hall immediately
following the ceremony.

Family and friends donated almost everything used in the wedding and reception. Chris' mom asked a co-worker to make the wedding cake. Since they were members of their church, a fee was not charged for the use of the church and fellowship hall. Also, since Pastor Glen considered himself a big brother to Rose, he didn't charge them to perform the wedding.

For the honeymoon, Chris had wanted to take Rose on a tour of the Blue Ridge and Smoky mountains, staying in cities like Pigeon Forge and Cherokee, but he couldn't afford it. Instead, he asked his aunt and uncle for the use of their cabin in Alabama. It was in the woods overlooking a lake. The nearest neighbor was several miles away. This would make it perfect for a honeymoon.

The only problem was that the cabin was not completed. It had floors, a ceiling, and walls. A bed was in one of the bedrooms, and the cabin also had a couch, black-and-white TV, coffee table, stove, oven, and a dining room table with chairs.

The electricity was connected, but Chris had to climb a ladder to put in the main fuse for the electricity to flow to the cabin. There was, however, no indoor plumbing. This didn't bother Chris any, but he wasn't certain how Rose would take it.

About twenty feet from the cabin was a pavilion that housed several picnic tables, a refrigerator, chest-type freezer, and another stove and oven. Up the hill behind the pavilion, a small outhouse sat hidden in the woods. The only source of running water was a spring coming out of the hillside in the woods.

His aunt and uncle had put a large hose into this spring. This hose carried water down the hill to the pavilion. At the pavilion, the hose connected with a

126

short PVC pipe that was connected to the side of a tree at one corner of the pavilion. The water emptied into a large wooden bucket. At the top of the bucket were two holes, out of which the water poured into a tiny ditch that took the water down to the lake. Hanging beside the bucket was a tin drinking cup.

Chris went by himself to buy some presents for Rose to open after the wedding. He bought a bikini (for her to use when they were alone, not in a public place, since it wouldn't be modest), a sundress, and several pieces of lingerie.

He was a little embarrassed to be shopping in the women's sections for the bikini and sundress, but he was **really** embarrassed to be shopping for lingerie. He didn't want anyone thinking he was a transvestite. If he were already married, he could flash a wedding ring and not feel so embarrassed, but now he just had to suffer the humiliation and stares.

He was getting disgusted with the selection of lingerie. Almost everything looked "slutty" and "trampy," which did not appeal to him. Finally, he swallowed his male pride and asked the saleslady for help. She asked him what he had in mind, to which he replied, "Something soft and feminine, but sexy. I want her to look like a lady, not a tramp."

"I think I know what you are talking about. You want something white with a lot of satin and lace."

"Yeah! Do you have anything like that?" he asked the J. C. Penny Outlet saleslady. She took him away from the rest of the lingerie to a display by itself and showed him exactly what he had in mind. Like Rose, it was very pure and lady-like.

He wrapped all the presents and had them ready for the honeymoon. Before the wedding, however, he had to finish all of his finals at school. Also, Gordon was a two-year college, and he would be graduating. The graduation ceremony would be in the middle of his honeymoon. He decided that the honeymoon was more important, so he just had the diploma mailed to him.

He finished the last final, then emptied his room and headed to Douglasville. The very next day would be the wedding day.

Chris and his brother, Bill, moved furniture and tables to set up the church and fellowship hall the morning of the wedding. Then they drove the hour and a half to the cabin to get it ready for that night, even arranging the presents in a spiraled pyramid shape. They were running late, and still had to have showers and get dressed.

They rushed back to Douglasville, "bending" the speed limit a teeny bit. They took turns showering and then hurried to the church.

Rose had been there some time. She had gotten her hair done that afternoon, and was now dressed in the wedding gown, getting made-up by one of Grandmother's daughters, whom Rose called Aunt Cindy.

Rose and Chris had bought the bridal bouquet from a store in town that was going out of business, so they got an excellent deal on it. Chris' mom made the rest of the flowers for the wedding. Rose's dress did not come with a veil, so she had to borrow one. One of Chris' cousins, who is in law enforcement, and at the time took crime scene photos, volunteered to be the photographer. Chris thinks that he and Rose were the first <u>live</u> subjects that his cousin had photographed.

A few minutes before the wedding was supposed to start, this cousin informed Rose that Chris had not yet arrived at the church. She began to worry that he wasn't coming.

Chris pulled into the church parking lot about two minutes before the wedding was supposed to start. His shirt wasn't buttoned fully, and he didn't have his tie on (the Marines had taught him how to tie a tie). He still had to get a few last things prepared before the wedding.

Chris was more nervous than he had ever been. He kept trying to find things to do to make sure the wedding was perfect, until Pastor Glen made him stand in a closet to one side of the platform until it was time for Chris and him to come out for the start of the ceremony.

Rose was absolutely beautiful. Chris could see her somewhat through the veil, since it wasn't a thick one. She looked as nervous as Chris. Paw-paw gave her away.

Rose and Chris exchanged glances, letting each other know they were glad to be getting married, but still nervous at going through the ceremony. One of Pastor Glen's daughters-in-law sang "You Needed Me" for Rose, and Bill read a poem that Chris had written about marriage. Instead of a unity candle, Chris and Rose decided to have Communion.

Chris had always thought weddings took too long, until his own. He was so happy during the wedding that it seemed to be over in seconds. "Is that it?" he thought to himself.

He was so happy to "kiss the bride," realizing that they were <u>finally</u> married. They were both proud to be announced as Mr. and Mrs. Chris Jarrell.

The reception did seem to take too long. Chris' friends made a circle around him, making it impossible for him to walk around and thank everyone else for coming and/or helping with the wedding. This angered some of Chris' relatives, but there was nothing he could do about it.

They were glad when it was finally time to leave for the honeymoon. Chris hadn't let Rose change into another dress. He wanted her to keep on her wedding gown—don't ask why.

As they were leaving, one of the flower girls was crying because she didn't get to throw any birdseed at Chris and Rose. Rose told her she could throw some, and bent over expecting a few seeds gently thrown. Instead, Rose got a face full of seed thrown as hard as the little girl could throw it. Rose had birdseed in her nose, mouth, and hair. She was now the one crying (for pain).

Finally underway, Chris stopped to get gas and a car wash at the Shell station on Highway 5, about fifteen minutes away. He had been driving by bending low and looking between letters made of shaving cream. He was afraid that just by turning on the wipers, it would only smear the shaving cream, and he wouldn't be able to see at all. Besides, there were paper streamers tied from bumper to bumper.

The manager gave them the free car wash they got for filling up their tank, plus gave them another one as a wedding present. The next stop would be the cabin. Rose was worried about two things, though. First, she wasn't looking forward to unpacking all their stuff in their new apartment after the honeymoon. Chris' brother and sisters were secretly getting things ready for them to surprise Rose when Chris would carry her over the threshold of their first home together.

The second thing that worried Rose was that she was still concerned that she would not satisfy Chris sexually as Linda had not been able to do for Jerry. She thought about that the whole way to the cabin. Satan gets people like Jerry to tell those who are insecure that they are "no good," or "useless," or that they will "never be good for anything." Then, he whispers to their minds that they are inadequate until they get so worried about it, even believing Satan's lies, that they begin feeling and acting as if it were true. They are so afraid that other people will not like them, or will be disappointed with them, that they cannot even enjoy the good times or good things that happen to them. This was happening to Rose. She couldn't fully enjoy the wedding or the reception for fear of being a failure— of disappointing the one she loved most in this world, Chris.

Rose was really surprised by the cabin. She liked not having any close neighbors, and loved the view of the lake from the bedroom window. She didn't mind not having running water. She just made Chris go get pots full of water, which she would heat on the stove for a sponge bath. Chris "showered" in the spring water running out of the bucket, freezing all the while. Rose didn't like the outhouse, though.

Upon arrival, Rose was surprised by the mound of presents. She was almost at tears with every present. Of all the presents Chris purchased, Rose's favorite present was the elegant gown that the J. C. Penny saleslady helped Chris find.

Rose insists that the present that meant the most of all those Chris gave to her was his virginity. She was the only one with whom he had shared himself. No other person can truthfully claim to have had sex with Chris, which makes Rose feel all the more loved and special.

Chris insists that Rose was worth the wait. He did not understand why God didn't want him to have sex with the girl that tried to seduce Chris around age twelve, until he met Rose. Then, he was glad he had kept himself pure for her. To him, his virginity was also the greatest gift he could give to Rose. He had kept himself pure for nineteen years. He had not kept anything else for that long to give to Rose, and nothing was so much a part of him as his own body.

Later that night, as they were falling asleep, Chris hugged Rose, kissing her on the top of the head. "You satisfy me, Rose," he assured her. She would not have to worry about it again.

EPILOGUE

After over eight years of marriage and four children, Rose and Chris are still married and more in love than they were when they got married. They still act like newlyweds, and still want to spend time together as much as they can. Why are they doing so well when many marriages today fail in the first five years? The answer is in a letter Chris wrote to Rose before he even asked her to marry him:

12-3-91

My beloved,

I was just reading in my psychology book—studying for my final tomorrow. I think I finally figured out why I love you so much and how God made our love and our relationship so strong. It is like people keep saying—the most important thing in a relationship is to be friends first in everything. That's it!

I love you so much because you're my best friend. You really are—more that anyone else, you are my friend. The book was talking about how important it is for a person to talk to someone else and release their fears, tell experiences, and relate failures, achievements, goals, desires, and wishes. It talked about how relieved a person feels to tell everything that a person holds inside to another privately and is still accepted by that person. Even when I tell you I failed or did something I am ashamed of, you still care about me. I love you for that. Thank you. You are my best friend.

A mutual friend of Rose and Chris would not date a friend of hers because she didn't "feel" anything, saying there was "no chemistry." She started seeing people who would use her just for sex and leave her. She even committed adultery with a married co-worker.

Through all this, the man about whom she felt no "chemistry" would sit and listen to her stories of sin and the hurt in her heart. He is a sincere Christian and wanted to be her boyfriend (and possible husband) because she had once been a Christian and he hoped she would repent of her sins and return to God. He loved her in his heart. He knew her faults, and loved her anyway, but she refused to try to love him because she thinks love is an emotion, a feeling, or sexual attraction, not a commitment. She doesn't understand what true love is—a commitment.

The marriage that will last is a marriage where the relationship is not based on sex, "feeling," or "chemistry." The marriage that will last is a marriage where the relationship is based on friendship—the commitment to be friends no matter what. This man would be perfect for her because he is already her friend, despite knowing the horrible depths to which she has fallen. If she would open her eyes, she would discover like the song by Survivor states, "The search is over. Love was right before my eyes."

How was Rose able to trust men after what Jerry had done to her? Chris had once told her, "I'm so glad you didn't become a homosexual after what he did to you. A lot of homosexuals became homosexuals because they were sexually abused. They couldn't trust the opposite sex after that happened to them. How come you decided not to become a homosexual?"

"It would have been so easy," Rose admitted. "But I couldn't do that. I love Jesus too much. Jerry hurt His heart by what he did to me. How could I hurt God's heart even more by becoming a homosexual? Besides, I still liked men. I didn't blame all of them just because Jerry was no good. That wouldn't have been fair or right."

Forgiveness is necessary for a person's emotional and physical health, but also for spiritual well being. Jesus said that if we do not forgive others, neither will our Father in Heaven forgive us for our sins.

In other words, unforgiveness toward others can keep you from going to heaven. Forgiveness does not mean that you allow a criminal to go unprosecuted, because an unrepentant criminal could hurt someone else. You can forgive by not holding a grudge, and by letting the criminal justice system take over.

If you are a man or woman, boy or girl, and have ever been harmed by another person—whether through sexual abuse and rape like Rose, or from a drunk driver's carelessness, or any of a thousand or more ways for one person to harm another—please, forgive the one who harmed you. You will feel better about yourself and others, and can start to put your life back together.

Marriage won't solve all your problems, though. Rose still struggles with self-esteem. Getting married did not stop it. Marriage will not make Chris and Rose's friend a faithful wife. Only God can do that, and then only when the person trusts God as Savior <u>and</u> Lord. When the person surrenders to God and His leading, only then can the sinful nature be defeated and the person become a faithful spouse and past problems be solved. You can't do it on your own. Trust Jesus. He is waiting to be your Savior and Lord. Ask Him to come into your life and save you today. Surrender to Him today. He will never do anything that is not for your ultimate good. Jesus loves you, this I know, for the Bible tells me so.

ABOUT THE AUTHORS

Rosalee Jarrell and **T. Christopher Jarrell** have been happily married for over eight years. They are raising four precious children—three girls and one boy. Rose is a graduate of Hart County High School in Hartwell, Georgia. Chris graduated from Jasper County High School in Monticello, Georgia. Later, he received an A. S. in Business Administration from Gordon College in Barnesville, Georgia. He also holds a Bachelor in Pastoral Ministries from Toccoa Falls College in Toccoa Falls, Georgia.

Though they are white, Chris proudly holds a "License to Minister" from a non-denominational, African-American association of churches. Together, Rose and Chris pastor Jesus' Church For All People in Penfield, Georgia. The church is "A non-denominational, interracial, multicultural church with one message: salvation comes through faith in Jesus Christ alone." Chris also writes, for the Greensboro, Georgia *Herald Journal* newspaper, a weekly article entitled "Thus Saith The Lord...," in which he addresses current events and issues from a Biblical perspective.

For speaking engagements, please write to PO Box 1311; Greensboro, GA 30642.

www.ingramcontent.com/pod-product-compliance
Lightning Source LLC
Chambersburg PA
CBHW051422280526
45785CB00003B/1126